# STERN RULES!

**The Seven Rules of Business Everyone Can Learn From Howard Stern**

**By Jamie Troia**

Copyright © 2012 by James Troia. All Rights Reserved.

First Edition

Published by Greystack Partners, LLC

To book Jamie Troia for a speaking engagement, visit
www.greystack.com

This book has not been read, approved, sponsored, or licensed by Howard Stern.

Back Cover Photograph: Kristen Memmolo

All rights reserved.  No part of this book may be reproduced or transmitted in any form or by any means, electronic or mechanical, including photocopying, recording, or by any information storage and retrieval system without written permission from the author, except for the inclusion of brief quotations in a review.

Limit of Liability/Disclaimer of Warranty: While the publisher and author have used their best efforts in preparing this book, they make no representations or warranties with respect to the accuracy or completeness of the contents of this book and specifically disclaim any implied warranties of merchantability or fitness for a specific purpose. No warranty may be created or extended by sales representatives or written sales materials.  The advice, strategies, and ideas expressed in this work may not be suitable for your situation.  You should consult with a professional where appropriate.  Neither the publisher nor author shall be liable for any loss of profit or any other commercial damages, including but not limited to special, incidental, consequential, or other damages.

To Howard Stern and the Staff of
*The Howard Stern Show,*
Thanks for working so hard to make mornings more enjoyable for millions of people. It worked.

# ACKNOWLEDGMENTS

I'd like to thank Danielle Troia, Jonathan Troia, Jackie Troia, Joe Troia, Judy Troia, Joe Rand, Greg Rand, Matt Rand, Rob Grosser, Roger & Kristen Memmolo, and Josh Baty

I must also acknowledge my friend and college roommate, Keith Stinton, whose promise that this book would never get made, pushed me when I doubted it myself.

# CONTENTS

Introduction ..................................................................... 7

My Stern Superfan Story ............................................... 11

Rule #1: Building a Brand is Personal: All Hail the King of All Media ........................................................... 15

Rule #2: If It's Your Job, Just F'ing Do It! .................... 35

Rule #3: Don't Be a *Phony.* Honesty, Honesty, Honesty! ......................................................................... 53

Rule #4: Cut through the Noise: The Art of the Live Read ................................................................................. 73

Rule #5: Obsessive Passion Is Contagious ................ 93

Rule #6: Have the Loyalty of an English Bulldog ..... 105

Rule #7: Demand Originality and Innovation ............ 127

Conclusion: An "Honest" Interview............................ 137

About the Author.......................................................... 147

"Howard Stern has built a powerful empire and brand through cunning business decisions and attention-getting publicity. Stern Rules! pulls from Howard's successes in business, and summarizes each powerful lesson into a quick, easy, and fun, read for Stern fans and non-fans alike."
*Jim F. Kukral - Author of Attention! This Book Will Make You Money*

"I am a lifelong entrepreneur and Howard fan, but until Jamie wrote Stern Rules! I had no idea how connected those two things were. It's about time Howard got credit for being the business and leadership genius he is, if for nothing else, getting so much productivity out of Baba Booey."
*Greg Rand, CEO OwnAmerica & Author Crash/Boom*

# Introduction

*Stern Rules!* is a collection of observations garnered over the past twenty years of listening to Howard Stern while trying to "make it" in the business world—a business world that, for me, shifted as radically as Howard's career during the same time frame.

In some cases, there are correlations in the arc of Howard's career and mine, and in other cases, not so much. Both of us dealt with a large conglomerate. In Howard's case, it was NBC, in my case, GE, which purchased NBC in 1986, shortly after Howard was fired in 1985. Both of us could not find a home among the "this is the way we have always done it, and this is the way it will continue to be done" mentality.

I get the feeling Howard has long been in search of a place where he could feel "at home." Therapy, a five-year renewal with Sirius satellite radio signed in 2010, and a prime-time gig on NBC's *America's Got Talent* might indicate that he's close, but anyone who listens to Howard knows that feeling one hundred percent "at home" will probably never happen for him.

His entrance into satellite radio was a huge,

bold break from the establishment and a way to have a greater say in plotting his own course. That is in many respects the same path that I have taken to end up as a strategy, technology, and marketing consultant.

The need to own the road may be one of the reasons I have long felt a kinship with a man that I have never met and why I have admired, respected, and been entertained by him for more than two decades.

*Stern Rules!* has in no way been approved, sponsored, or licensed by Howard Stern. In fact, despite my efforts, I would be surprised if he knows that it exists.

I hope that the book makes enough of an impact on people that Howard publically acknowledges his valid and unique approach to running a business. He deserves recognition much in the same way that Donald Trump, Mark Zuckerberg or any other modern day, self-made man in the public spotlight deserves recognition for his business acumen. Howard has a media empire where he leaves his mark on nearly every detail and where the culture is defined by the personality of its leader.

The fact that Howard doesn't "own" the company is a small matter. In fact, it may speak to his talent, perseverance, and skill that he has managed to become one of the country's highest-paid entertainers while collecting a paycheck from a media company run by others.

I've done my best to bring Howard's approach to business to life, but a "super fan" and business man can draw only so many insights in a vacuum.

Howard has spoken about Malcolm Gladwell's "ten thousand hours of greatness" rule. In his book, *Outliers*, Gladwell discusses how ten thousand hours of practicing something seem to be required to achieve greatness.

Looking back at my career and interest changes over the years, I know I've spent ten thousand hours listening to *The Howard Stern Show*. I put my training to the test with *Stern Rules!*

I hope that one day Howard will recognize that this is a business story that needs to be told from his perspective as well. I hope he has the time and inclination to do it.

**Thanks, and a Baba Booey to y'all!**

# My Stern Superfan Story

I've listened to Howard since I was in high school when I'd listen to his show in a '72 Nova on the way home from school with my friends.

Once high school was over and I went to college outside Stern's radio coverage area and I couldn't wait for the summer so that I could take a plumbing assistant job and listen to Howard all morning. I had always admired his sense of humor, honesty, and way of making me feel like part of the show.

This admiration led me to wake up one cool, April morning in Albany, New York and do my best to see Howard win the nomination for governor of New York.

The atmosphere outside the Italian American Center in Albany was electric. After slugging down a few freshly mixed Bloody Marys in a parking lot littered with hundreds of other Stern fans, I positioned myself in front of Howard's bus while he addressed the crowd.

Although his comments were everything you would expect to hear from Howard, I heard determination in his voice. It seemed that Howard really wanted the governorship.

As his crew exited the bus and headed into the Italian-American Center to attend the nomination proceedings, I latched onto the end of the line. Feeling like a true wack-packer (a wack-packer is a *Stern Show* guest that typically has some physical or mental challenge but is a dedicated Howard Stern fan), I marched into the secured building behind Howard's staff, Fred Norris, Baba Booey, Jackie the Jokeman, and the Stern entourage.

Once inside, Howard addressed the crowd while live on the air, and that was the moment when I had my one and only interaction with Howard.

As Howard addressed the crowd, he seemed to be searching for the right words to describe his gubernatorial run. During his rant, as I stood in front of Fred and Jackie, Howard seemed to be searching for someone to compare himself to. It was April 23, 1994, one day after President Nixon died. Knowing that Howard liked to relate to current events, I blurted, "Like Nixon!"

Howard glanced in my direction and belted out something along the lines of "Yes, like Richard Nixon."

For years, I had heard Jackie and Fred feed Howard lines from behind the scenes and thought that I could be there with them. That day, I was there, and had a split second interaction with Howard that ended up on air. Man, I would love to have a copy of the audio of that show so that I could see if my memory is in line with reality.

*If you have a "Stern Superfan" story, I want to hear from you. I am assembling stories and essays from Stern fans about their chance meetings with him, the crazy stunts they've pulled in an effort to meet the "King of All Media," and how he has affected their lives. Visit SternRules.com to submit your story for inclusion in my next book.*

# Rule #1:
# Building a Brand is Personal: All Hail the King of All Media

Howard Stern is the King of All Media. The title not only suits him but has become synonymous with him. I've never heard anyone else refer to himself using that title. It's Howard's, he owns it, and it's a good title in the world of show business.

Let's not forget that the beauty of this lofty title lies in the fact that Howard was self-crowned. No one bestowed the title upon him — he took it, like any good king!

He has always had an extremely keen sense of personal branding. He has moved in a calculated manner to develop his brand and the persona that he wants to portray, but his approach has always been authentic.

*"The secret to my show is honesty, reality, that I will say the truth."*
- Howard Stern on *The O'Reilly Factor*, 12/2005

Long before Twitter and Facebook, Howard was on the airwaves building a brand. He has mentioned that bringing the audience into his thought process was an important element of his show and his success.

His approach to notoriety was to push the envelope of broadcasting standards. He pushed the limits of language on the air, often receiving warnings and fines from the Federal Communications Commission (FCC). He pushed the limits of content by dreaming up sexually charged "games" for his studio guests to play. In inventing the rules of these games, he saw just how far (or low) people would go to get on the radio.

Testing the limits in every way possible was a key element to Howard's brand development, but like all great brands, the "Stern brand" evolved over the years. It's often mentioned on the show that when people in mainstream media talk about Howard, they use words like "vulgar," "shocking," and "outrageous."

Howard has discussed how the broader media draw conclusions on who he is based on what he was like ten years ago or on what people hear and say about him. He built a strong brand in the 1990s, and he still carries many of the "brand attributes" that he established then, even though he and the show have changed.

Despite the changes that have taken place, the "Howard Stern brand" that was built around having attractive, naked women in the studio, fart jokes, and in-studio games like "anal ring toss" is cemented in the public consciousness. Cemented to the point that it appears that even Howard himself has found it difficult to modify this perception in mainstream America.

How has his brand shifted since the crazy days of the 1990s? He transitioned his show into one where listeners tune in to hear the most honest celebrity interviews anywhere. His ability to capture bigger stars for interviews and his honest political and social commentary has (in large part) replaced the outrageous bits and super-hot lesbians.

I'd say that he is now faced with the challenge of transforming his brand to match the transformation of his show and I'm guessing that he is banking on his appearance on NBC TV's *America's Got Talent* in prime-time will help.

Howard is using social media to mold his brand into something more mainstream. His million-plus followers on Twitter follow him because of his years on the radio, but now he is using the platform to pull those listeners into *America's Got Talent*.

## Be Your Own King

In today's fast-paced, social media-enabled world, the concept of building a personal brand is gaining steam and creeping into the public consciousness.

The term "personal branding" is thought to have been first used in 1997 by Tom Peters. His book, *In Search of Excellence*, was required reading for my college's business program, and I suspect that it was for many others in the late 1980s.

"Building your brand" is about creating equity in and around who you are. You don't need to be famous, run a company, or be outgoing to build a brand. You build your brand every day whether you like it or not. If you show up late for work every day, it factors into your brand. If you show up with Starbucks coffee every morning, you're building a different brand than if you show up with coffee from Dunkin Donuts.

You build your brand in meetings, on phone calls, and at happy hour. Some people recognize this and manage their brand, and some don't. Don't confuse building your brand with portraying yourself as something that you're not. That's the quickest way to "kill your brand."

Building your brand involves determining what you want to be known for and actively managing that reputation, both in the real world and online.

The online world has brought the concept of personal branding to the forefront of our culture. As was said in the movie *The Social Network* (the story about Facebook's rise to fame), "The Internet isn't written in pencil… it's written in ink." Information about millions of Americans and most every business is now available online, and in many cases it will be there forever. The more content you create that's in line with what you want your brand to represent, the more people will see you in that light. If you talk the talk, you need to walk the walk.

It used to be that if you interviewed for a job or met prospective clients for the first time, all they knew about you was what you put in front of them—a resume, sales literature, or a proposal.

If the person you were meeting shared

contacts or business associates with you, he might be able to call a common associate to find out just what kind of person you are.

Today, people use Google and social networks to find you and find out what you are all about. They discover this information on their terms, not yours.

Recent news stories have discussed how some employers are asking prospective employees for their Facebook login credentials so that they can see personal profiles from the inside. This is scary stuff.

If you're not managing what people find out about you, you're leaving it up to chance. Actively manage your online profiles and present yourself in the way that you want people to see you.

Present the authentic *you*. You can't build an online persona that does not reflect who you are in the real world.

It's okay for your online profile to be a "larger than life" facsimile of the real you, but there needs to be authenticity and consistency between who you are and what people see when they communicate on sites like Facebook, Twitter, and LinkedIn.

## Build Your Own Kingdom

There has never been more tools to build a personal brand than there are today. Networking, blogs, and social media sites have given you a multitude of platforms to communicate with millions of people.

It used to be that people with a new vision for radio were forced to bust their ass at crappy radio stations, year in and year out, working their way up the ladder. The farther up the ladder they made it, the larger stations they worked for until they finally landed at a station with a signal strong enough to reach millions of people.

Howard Stern worked his ass off so that he could reach broader audiences, as defined by the ratings his show got and the strength of the signal blasting from the top of the radio station building.

This is no longer the only way to reach an audience or build a fan base. It's not even the *best* way to do it anymore. The web has changed the game. In traditional forms of media, you had to pay your dues for years in order to break through and give people access to your ideas. Now, you can achieve a breakthrough nearly instantly.

## Books versus E-books

Twenty-five years ago, if you wanted to write a book, you pulled out your twenty-five-pound Smith Corona (that's a typewriter), typed a hundred or so pages of your best work, made fifty photocopies of the manuscript, went to the library and found the addresses of the top publishing companies, mailed your manuscript to those companies, and then waited for your rejection letters.

People who want to establish their brand using the power of the written word have much more power today. Discussions are taking place about whether the publishers who held all the power ten or fifteen years ago even have a place in the future of publishing. Talk about a seismic shift.

In today's world, you can write your book on a light-as-air laptop computer weighing less than three pounds, never once having to pull out the correction fluid to fix an errant keystroke. Once your book is complete, you have infinite ways to promote and sell your work.

In addition to promotion through blogs, Facebook, Twitter, and other social media sites, you can post your e-book on Amazon and make it immediately available from the largest book retailer in the world, one that has a website instead of a real storefront and whose customers use pencil-thin book readers to purchase and download books, every second of every day.

## Radio versus Podcasts

Could Howard have benefited from podcast technology twenty years ago?

We can debate whether the struggles that Howard took on during the course of his career made him a better broadcaster in the long run. There is no doubt that constantly fighting with competing disc jockeys to reach the top of his profession helped to make him who he is today.

As someone who believed in himself so strongly and who has discussed his burning desire to be on the radio from the age of five, Howard may well have benefited from being able to produce and distribute a global radio show from his bedroom as a teenager . Using podcast technology, a young Howard Stern could record his show through his computer and make it available for download to millions of people across the Internet.

What would have happened if he didn't have to take crappy $96-a-week jobs in lousy radio stations? Imagine if podcasts were so prevalent twenty years ago that he didn't have to dodge program managers, station directors, and the FCC?

What kind of world would it be if he had total creative freedom from day one and the tools to build an audience? How might his show have been different in the late 1980s and early 1990s? What new ground would have been broken?

We'll never know, but we do know that there are literally thousands of talented, upstart broadcasters who, with laptops and microphones, are creating "radio programs" that our world has never heard. These can range from programs with broad appeal such as newscasts and comedy to specific, tight-niche shows that could never have been made prior to today's technology.

## Newspapers versus Blogs

When I was a kid, it seemed like there was a new TV show every week about a young, upstart journalist who wanted to make it as a newspaper reporter. Jimmy Olsen and Lois

Lane in *Superman* were rehashed over and over.

Today, Lois Lane would probably have a blog called ManofSteelUpdate.com and be building her own audience rather than the readership of *The Daily Planet* for Perry White.

Blogs represent the foundation of the shift that we see in new media. The success of blogs has in some measure been attributed to their ability to grant readers the ability to comment and interact with the writer's original post. In many ways, *The Howard Stern Show* has many similarities to a blog. Howard expresses his thoughts on a range of topics in a thoughtful and honest way. During the radio show, he takes listeners' phone calls, and the listeners get to comment on the content that they've been presented.

The conversation continues even after he has moved on to new ideas.

## Television and Movies versus YouTube and Netflix

Of all the shifts in media, video content is the biggest game changer. Never before could video producers have instant access to millions of users within minutes of completing their content. Websites like YouTube allow people to post videos to a platform that has become the web's second-largest search engine.

Netflix, a company that found success by focusing on efficiently sending and receiving DVDs via U.S. Mail, now provides access to its content by building their interface into millions of devices and is now creating its own custom programming. It is in essence creating its own television network on the Internet.

## Who Will Dethrone the King?

Howard Stern is considered by many of his fans to be a "regular" guy who had a voice in the media and grew his audience slowly and systematically. Now that social media and social networks give anyone a voice and access to millions of potential listeners, the playing field has been leveled. We'll see more and more engaging and entertaining personalities emerge. Who might these personalities be? We've seen people emerge as pseudo-celebrities from viral YouTube videos, and we've learned about people who have used technology as a vehicle to fame and made a boatload of money.

Gary Vaynerchuk of the Wine Library in New Jersey used social media and video to increase the sales of his parents liquor store five or six hundred percent in just a few years. He is now a speaker, bestselling author, and social media consultant who makes thousands of dollars for speaking to audiences, freely dropping "f-bombs" and other words that Howard could get away with only on satellite radio.

Who will emerge as a mainstream Internet celebrity? Why not you?

## Truth Sets You Free

Although social media platforms are extremely powerful communication devices, there are rules that, if not followed, will likely have you talking to yourself instead of a legion of raving fans. Make no mistake—the ability to create that legion of fans is real and infinitely achievable provided that you go about in the right fashion and with a specific goal in mind.

Building a personal brand has different value for different people, and it can take various forms, depending on your goals. For some, the goal is to shift their real-world reputation, influence, and skills to the online world. Others are looking to carve out an online niche, to make an impact, and become more memorable by creating an "on-air" persona that gets people's attention.

If there is an element to personal branding that virtually all experts agree is *the* critical component, it is authenticity. Authenticity has long been a key component of Howard's brand and will likely remain a key to the success of his radio show.

In our society, people are more skeptical than ever. They work to determine the authenticity of a person or message quickly. If their initial reaction to you is that you are full of shit, you don't get a second chance.

If you come across as real, people often stick around to hear what's next. Here's the hard fact I've learned about establishing trust with your audience, customers, or prospects: the trust that took years to establish can vanish in seconds.

You build trust by applying layer upon layer of goodwill. If you are consistent and continue to provide your audience with useful (or entertaining) information, you continue to build your brand and trust.

If you purposefully or even accidentally violate that trust, you will likely destroy everything you have worked so hard to build.

Treat your reputation as one of your most valuable assets. Protect it as such, because if you lose it, you'll be spending all your time trying to rebuild it rather than moving your business or career forward.

## The "Private Parts" Phenomenon

It took Howard more than ten years to build

his audience to the point where a company like Simon and Schuster felt that he was bankable enough to publish his first book, *Private Parts*. Even getting an endorsement from what many would consider to be the most influential publisher in the world didn't cause him to lose sight of his audience.

Always the promoter (I've heard him refer to being like P. T. Barnum when discussing self-promotion), Howard announced to his legions of fans that he would go on a national book tour in support of *Private Parts*.

That in and of itself probably didn't surprise anyone. Most celebrity authors, particularly those new to the publishing game, often commit to promote their book with in-store signings and other on-site promotions. This means that their handlers (managers, agents, and publishers) schedule a book-signing tour.

During the planning stages, the team identifies which cities will be visited, which bookstores will be included, when the signings start and end, and the logistics of whizzing the author off to the next city.

They may think, "How can we get our precious author in and out of these signings with as little stress and time commitment possible?"

Once the plan is put into action, it's not uncommon for the author to show up for the signing five to ten minutes late and leave thirty seconds after the signing is scheduled to end. They do the bare minimum.

Howard did things differently. He committed to a rigorous tour that covered more cities than many authors would consider. When he hit the airwaves in the mornings during his tour, he told his audience that he would not disappoint them. He promised his listeners that if they took time out of their busy lives to come to his book signing, their book would get signed, period. He proclaimed that the signing would not end until the last listener left the line with an autographed copy of *Private Parts*.

Talk about building trust. The benefits of this approach became clear when Howard visited Barnes and Noble on Fifth Avenue in New York for a signing, and ten thousand fans showed up to get their books signed by the King of All Media.

Howard's masterful promotion and his commitment to his loyal fan base resulted in the initial printing of *Private Parts*—two hundred and fifty thousand copies—selling out within hours of release. *Private Parts* quickly became the fastest-selling book in Simon and Schuster's history.

The book sold so fast that in two weeks, the book entered its eighth printing and had sold more than a million copies.

## Rule #1 Summary

Howard spent more than thirty years in radio building a brand that shattered the mold of what a radio DJ should be. Today, even as he has matured, he has stayed true to his core brand "promises." No matter what.

There are many new technologies that make building your brand easier than ever before. Keep the brand-building tactics that follow in mind, and you may someday be a "king" in your own right!

You build your personal brand every day by the actions you take. Craft your brand around how you want others to see you, and you'll begin to "act like your brand."

If you're not actively managing your brand and reputation, you leave them to chance. Make brand and reputation management part of your everyday life.

It's okay for your brand to evolve as long as it stays true to your core values. Many people have slammed Howard for "changing." He entertained people based on his core values of honesty and loyalty, and as long as he stays true to those values, his brand will successfully evolve.

Traditional methods of building a brand were often unapproachable for individuals and small companies. This is no longer the case. Traditional media has been transformed so that highly accessible complements to traditional media outlets that build brand awareness are available. Blogs, social media, e-books, online videos, and podcasts are the new tools for building brands, and they are readily available to everyone.

Authenticity drives success in brands. Don't be afraid to expose or even highlight your shortcomings. People will respect and trust you more if you don't claim to be perfect or all things to all people. There are areas where you suck—your audience knows it, and you know it. Sell them on your strengths, and they can overlook your weaknesses.

Suggested reading:
Bhargava, Rohit. *Personality Not Included: Why Companies Lose Their Authenticity--and How Great Brands Get It Back*. New York: McGraw-Hill, 2008.

Godin, Seth. *Purple Cow: Transform Your Business by Being Remarkable*. New York: Portfolio, 2003.

Stern, Howard. *Miss America*. New York: Regan, 1995

# Rule #2:
# If It's Your Job, Just F'ing Do It!

Over the years, *The Howard Stern Show* has grown from a morning radio show, operating out of tiny WNBC studio, to a media empire broadcasting more than a dozen different satellite radio shows all over the world. Howard's empire consists of two twenty-four-hour satellite radio stations that, in addition to supporting other entertainers and radio shows, include a full-time news department and an on-demand cable station dedicated to *The Howard Stern Show*. This meteoric growth has meant that Howard's brand and staff have grown at a pace rivaling that of explosive Internet companies.

How has *The Howard Stern Show* been able to accommodate such growth while maintaining the quality programming that its fans are used to? People. Despite the fact that if asked, Howard might say, in his self-deprecating manner, that the bar was set pretty low, the hiring practices established early in the show's history helped to maintain quality and consistent programming.

*The Howard Stern Show* has been littered with staff members who have little or no experience with broadcast radio. This trend toward hiring energy and enthusiasm over knowledge (or smarts) started with "Boy Gary" Dell'Abate, Howard's long-time producer. Prior to joining *The Howard Stern Show*, Gary was scraping together whatever he could for work, searching for any path that might lead him to something he could call a career. One of his early radio jobs was babysitting a computer-controlled, overnight radio show to ensure that nothing went wrong.

Gary got his big break when he was hired as an assistant to a traffic reporter at WNBC in New York. That job ultimately led him to work with Howard. To hear Gary tell the story in his memoir, *They Call Me Baba Booey*, his down-to-earth demeanor, complete lack of pretense, and enthusiasm for the position ultimately endeared him to *The Howard Stern Show* staff and led to his hiring.

Howard subsequently mentioned on the air how what he really wanted was someone with experience in production who could help him and Fred Norris write comedy sketches. The problem at the time was that Howard was granted a budget of $150 a week by WNBC management. At $150 a week, Gary was all Howard could afford, but the team loved Gary's enthusiasm.

Howard turned Gary "Baba Booey" Dell'Abate into perhaps the most well-known TV or radio producer in the country (despite his gargantuan teeth and generally dopey demeanor). Gary achieved this level of notoriety in the entertainment industry after being hired as a guy to do "grunt work" around the show.

## "Yes, Boss"

The trend of hiring self-motivated, enthusiastic staff, with little regard for experience, continued at *The Howard Stern Show*. It's possible that because Baba Booey worked his way up the Stern ranks and was responsible for many of the show's hiring decisions, he felt compelled to give unqualified but energetic candidates the benefit of the doubt based on his own experience.

You don't need to look far back into the annals of the show's history to see that many of the interns and staffers were enthusiastic if not all that experienced (and in some cases, not all that intelligent). Many of the show's interns and assistants were at one time or another big parts of the on-air show.

Unfortunately for many of them, the entertainment often stemmed from Howard's systematic breakdown of their personalities and making fun of their intelligence. What they lacked in experience, they made up for in dedication.

Fans of the show will remember interns and staffers like K. C. Armstrong, Mike Gange, and Steve Grillo. The names aren't all that important, but they all became dedicated "Stern guys." Staffers that fit this mold were one hundred percent dedicated to Howard and the show's success, and in return, he was dedicated to them. Howard went out of his way to dedicate his second book, *Miss America*, to his personal intern, Steve Grillo. Steve was famously responsible for preparing a baked potato each morning to Howard's discerning tastes.

Howard seems to want a team that will bring a certain passion to the show and to the halls of *The Howard Stern Show* offices. The interns' youthfulness brings a contagious energy that seems to spread like a virus throughout the staff.

## Take Enthusiasm over Experience

Hiring a self-motivated staff is one of the most important things you can do as a business leader. Jim Collins, the author of *Good to Great*, says that the companies that achieve the highest levels of performance focus on finding the right people before anything else. They build their team even before defining their business strategy, business goals, or tactics.

In his book *Full Engagement*, Brian Tracy echoes this sentiment by attributing 95 percent of a manager's success to his or her ability to select the right team members.

It generally doesn't matter what *kind* of job self-motivated people are doing—they still do it well. Even prior to the Internet bubble burst of the 1990s, venture capital firms openly admitted that, in most cases, they invested in a leader or management team, not necessarily a business idea or concept. A well-put-together team with talented individuals can "pivot" and work out issues associated with a flawed product or business model. They rise above and come up with something that works.

All great ideas run into unforeseen road blocks and rely on superior execution. Weak management teams bank on great ideas, and strong management teams execute on plans and adapt to changing conditions.

A solid team gives your organization a huge competitive advantage. You are equipped with smart, hard-working people who can go wherever needed to make money.

If one business model is not working, turn on a dime and adopt a new model. Your staff's internal desire to succeed changes the game.

Self-motivated employees don't need to be prodded to take on new challenges. They take the initiative to learn new technologies and skills and apply them to make your company better and more competitive.

## It's Your Job

It seems that Howard doesn't have the time or the inclination to be the motivator of his staff. If he needs to motivate them, they were the wrong staff.

Once your role is established on *The Howard Stern Show*, and you know your responsibilities, you're expected to perform at a high level.

Howard apparently adopted the philosophy that if you've accepted responsibility for doing a job, and someone is willing to pay you to do the job, you should take great pride in the work that you perform. If you are not willing to give it 100%, you shouldn't take the work.

If you did take the job, his motto was "just get it done." No bitching, no complaining. Get it done for your own good and for the greater good. Being self-motivated is a critical part of being on *The Howard Stern Show*.

I think back to 2002 when Howard interviewed a young woman who worked a sex phone hotline.

During a "test" call in which he portrayed the customer, he quickly took offense that Corrine (the phone sex operator) was being passive. Howard drove the call, and Corrine merely responded to his playful questions. She did not take control of the conversation. He wanted Corrine to step it up and initiate some sexual banter. He got frustrated with her and scolded her—somewhat joking but mostly serious—because he took great exception to her work ethic. He explained that if she accepted the job and was getting paid to do it, she needed to do it to the best of her ability and not just "go through the motions." He thought that she owed her employer more.

Howard echoed his "just f'ing do it" sentiment again in 2006. Prior to his launch on satellite radio, he was a guest on Fox News and interviewed by Sean Hannity. In that interview, he made his position clear about working hard regardless of your job or what your future held.

He spoke about CBS radio, which owned WXRK in New York, his employer prior to his move to satellite radio. CBS radio had filed a lawsuit against him (Howard probably felt that the allegations amounted to "sour grapes" that he was leaving the station). He seemed clearly frustrated by the lawsuit, even hurt. Like he felt he was being screwed with by CBS and they were not giving him the professional respect and courtesy that he had shown them throughout his career.

> *I spent twenty years at this company, the last fourteen months I was there, I could have pulled shenanigans. I could have called in sick, I could have not shown up. I didn't have to read all those live commercials. I could have screwed with them. I'm not that kind of guy. I am a straight shooter, you hire me to do a job, I'm going to do it for you.*
> - Howard Stern on *Hannity & Colmes* 3/2005

His bottom line is this: If you're given a job to do, *just f'ing do it*.

## Employee Dial-a-Date

It is easier to understand "Stuttering John" Melendez at a crowded press conference than it is to properly identify the people who will help make your business a success.

You have to be able to reliably match what is important to you and the organization with what is important to the prospective employee.

For example, if your organization is one where the workday starts at four in the morning and runs until one in the afternoon, don't hire people who want to socialize three or four nights a week or need to see their children off to school in the morning.

Too many people, particularly people who hire for small teams or small companies, rely on their gut instinct to identify the right candidate for a new position.

The routine goes something like this: Go to Craigslist, put up a job description for the position and wait for resumes to roll in. You may wonder if half the people who send you a resume bothered to even *read* the job description. You get people from all walks of life responding to just about every kind of job these days.

You weed through the abundance of crap, conduct a handful of phone interviews, speak to a few people in person, and hire the "best" person.

If you are a good judge of human nature, run a multi-million-dollar empire, and are an experienced interviewer, this method has a small chance for success. Otherwise, do your homework.

In *Full Engagement*, Brian Tracy promotes The Law of Three in hiring:

**Interview three candidates.** Doing face-to-face interviews with at least three candidates gives you a good sense of who is available for the position.

**Interview three times**. It's amazing what will come out of people's mouths the *third* time they meet with you. They start to feel more relaxed with your presence and confident in their position. This often leads them to reveal more about themselves than in previous meetings.

**Meet in three different places.** Changing venue often brings out different personality traits. Is the person subtly or even overtly rude to a coffee shop waiter? Does he help a mother get her baby stroller through the door? By changing the venue, you can uncover things that may not have been revealed in a conference room.

**Have three different interviewers.** It's important to get different perspectives on a prospect, so include members of your existing team in the hiring process. When your team members speak with your prospects, they may unearth perspectives that you may have missed.

Making the wrong hiring decisions will infect your team and limit its ability to execute a plan. This is especially true with small groups, where a new hire makes up a much greater percentage of the whole. The costs associated with hiring the wrong people can be as bad as (or worse than) the benefits of hiring the right people.

If you make a bad hiring decision—it happens to everyone—remedy the situation quickly before it becomes a major disruption to your team.

## Howard Makes a Change to His Core Team

Aside from when writer Jackie "The Jokeman" Martling left the show due to a contract dispute, there was one time when Howard needed to change his core team. It happened early in Howard's career, but when it happened, Howard acted swiftly and decisively.

Shortly after he began working at 92.3 K-Rock in New York, his budget was expanded, and he was told that he could add another writer to his team. At the time, he and Fred were the primary creative forces of the show.

Howard thought about who would fit in and decided that Steve Chaconas, an old friend and colleague during his time in Washington, DC at DC-101, would be a logical selection. He asked Steve to join the show and help write comedy bits and sketches.

Chaconas decided to take the position but also decided that rather than move his family to New York, he would commute each week.

Chaconas was coming to New York late Sunday night or early Monday morning, staying in New York for the week (reportedly choosing to initially stay at Fred's apartment) and going back to Washington when work ended on Friday. Howard quickly realized that he wanted a writer who was willing to commit to the show and would not be a distraction. After a few weeks, Howard let Chaconas know that it was not working out and that he would be replaced.

The search for a writer continued until Howard reached out to Jackie "The Jokeman" Martling. Jackie became the newest writer on The Howard Stern Show. For many years, Jackie provided off-the-cuff comments and fed Howard lines in countless situations that helped make the show funny and irreverent.

Howard showed the traits of a great leader. When confronted with uncomfortable issues with employees, act swiftly and with conviction. Having people on your team who don't fit can be death to a team.

You may find that your most solid, contributing team members lose enthusiasm because a team member who does not fit in is sucking up resources that could be deployed more efficiently elsewhere. Bad team members may become such a distraction that others wonder when they can get rid of this person and get back to work.

## Wack Packer or Super Genius?

If you're looking for team members who will "run through walls for you" and do whatever it takes to get a job done, measure them on multiple criteria and across a spectrum of skills. If you are not a master at analyzing personality traits, a formal personality evaluation, something like Myers Briggs, helps to keep the selection process more objective and makes it easier to compare one candidate with another.

By profiling your prospects' personality tendencies, you can look objectively at their passions, values, and desires. You uncover conscious and subconscious motivations. What truly drives them? What financial gain, lifestyle need, career fulfillment, or other motivation gets them up in the morning? Once you have the results on paper, it makes it easier to evaluate your prospect for the position you are trying to fill as well as how the person will fit into the organization as a whole.

In many cases, companies search for many people with a specific personality profile. These are often instances where multiple people do the same type of job, such as on a national sales team.

If you have not identified the personality attributes of the position beforehand, you can get a sense of what the person is like based on testing and then determine whether or not there is a fit with the people they will interact with on a daily basis.

Use social networking sites like LinkedIn to assist in evaluating your prospects. Identify whether they have connections that you can contact in addition to the references they provide.

Look for characteristics in their background that might enhance their ability to thrive in your company. Are they a proven self-starter? Is there a history of success?

If a person doesn't have experience specific to your industry, does the candidate's background indicate that he or she can quickly adapt to different industries, technologies, and environments?

Many hiring managers make the mistake of matching a candidate's qualifications only with the needs for a specific position. They overlook the big picture and the person's ability to adapt to the culture.

Imagine that Robin Ophelia Quivers left *The Howard Stern Show* and you were tasked with finding a replacement news anchor. Imagine that you didn't know much about *The Stern Show*, but you knew network news.

If Tom Brokaw's resume came across your desk, it would be a slam-dunk hire, right? A twenty-year veteran of a network news show could certainly handle a position reporting the news on satellite radio.

I can see it now. Brokaw walks into the studio on his first day:

Stern: "Tom, did you get laid last night?"

Brokaw: (silence)

Stern: "Well, Tom, I tell you, my wife was out of town last night, but I was so horny I just had to masturbate to some babysitter porn. Do you know what babysitter porn is, Tom?"

Brokaw: "Um, today in Afghanistan, two U.S. soldiers were injured when…"

Stern: "Tom, screw Afghanistan, I'm talking about porn where the daddy comes home and gets it on with the babysitter! Is that hot or what? I'm telling you I came in like two seconds."

It wouldn't take long to realize that the cultural fit wasn't there.

I believe it is that cultural fit has helped Howard remain dedicated to Robin for so long. She was put in the "Brokaw chair" but she embraced the culture that Howard was building and she played off it. Robin helped empower him by going along with whatever he dreamed up. She could laugh at Howard's commentary and not be offended by it.

When hiring your staff, keep a keen eye out for the right fit and the right personality types, and you'll be sure to get more Baba Booeys and fewer Fafa Flunkys.

## Rule #2 Summary

Howard built a core team of professionals that for the most part, stayed intact throughout his rise to fame. As others came and went, the core team tackled new opportunities as they arose. Howard didn't have a magic formula when building his team; he picked people who shared his passion and people he liked. The following principles will help you build a team that you can hold onto for the long haul.

- Hire enthusiasm over experience. Passionate employees can work in any kind of business. Experienced people may be able to hit the ground running, but they are often set in their ways and won't innovate.
- Don't take a job unless you are willing to give it one hundred percent. The person "on the other end" of your paycheck is counting on you to deliver results. You were hired to do a job, be sure to deliver.
- Don't let hiring happen by accident. Put together a legitimate process, and stick to it. Follow the rule of three: meet three candidates, give three interviews, hold interviews in three locations, and let three people interview prospects.
- If you make a bad hire, fix it quickly.

Nothing will destroy a well-functioning team faster than someone who doesn't fit in. That doesn't mean that you need to hire a "yes man" or "yes woman." It means that if there is no cultural fit or people can't meet expectations, they need to go before they poison your culture.

- Personality screening may sound "touchy-feely" and not sit well with business traditionalists, but it is legit. Get objective assessments of people and their communication styles before you bring them on board.

Suggested reading:
Tracy, Brian. *Full Engagement!: Inspire, Motivate, and Bring out the Best in Your People*. New York: American Management Association, 2011.

Collins, James C. *Good to Great: Why Some Companies Make the Leap--and Others Don't*. New York, NY: Harper Business, 2001.

Dell'Abate, Gary, and Chad Millman. *They Call Me Baba Booey*. New York: Spiegel & Grau, 2010.

# Rule #3:
# Don't Be a *Phony*.
# Honesty, Honesty, Honesty!

Howard has used honesty as his rallying cry, as his shelter from censorship, and as the basis for his media empire.

> *"I've always been honest. One thing about— You don't have to like my radio show. There are those that like it and there are those that hate it. But one thing anyone who's ever heard my show knows, I'm a straight shooter, and I'm an honest guy."*
> - Howard Stern on *Hannity & Colmes* 3/2005

Every listener has come to expect honesty and authenticity from Howard and his team. Listeners are not subjected to drummed up, "made for radio" characters. We experience the trials and tribulations of real, authentic people. These people come on the air with real feelings, faults, and relationships. The authenticity of *The*

*Howard Stern Show* has helped Howard cultivate and maintain his audience for more than thirty years.

He removes the filters between entertainer and fan, and is one of the first to provide an honest glimpse into the world of fame. That idea does not seem all that revolutionary, does it?

Today, reality TV has taken over virtually every television network. These shows regularly break down the walls between entertainment and reality. They take us inside worlds and professions that we could never get a glimpse of before reality programming came into vogue.

Want to know the inside scoop on the restaurant business? There are about ten shows for you to watch. The art of tattoos? There are a few on that. Hunting alligators? Raising kids? Training dogs? Finding a mate? Pitching an investment? Making it as a singer, actor, or model? You better get your TiVo ready. You're in for a long night!

These shows have taken over programming. They're a network's dream. They're low-cost, short-turnaround programming that turn niche markets into national phenomena. Amazingly, as reality TV matures, it seems less real and more staged. It may come to the point where once again *The Howard Stern Show* is the measuring stick for "reality programming."

It's not grandstanding when Howard claims to be the pioneer of reality programming. He was among the first to create programming that judged guests with brutal honesty. He has long conducted beauty contests and talent shows with regular people off the street and given them an honest assessment of their assets.

He was also the first to allow people to view the inner workings of a radio show.

Unlike many other disc jockeys Howard never hid the fact that there were people on his staff who helped the show come to life. In fact, he invited them into the studio, put them on microphone, and gave listeners insight into their personalities. He humanized them for us, thus humanizing the show and making it approachable to anyone who listened.

He makes his listeners feel like they are *part* of the show. We are part of it because we are represented by other fans when they call in to speak to Howard and the gang and because we feel like we know what's going on behind the scenes.

The show is like a running soap opera. If you listen every day, you are "in on the joke." I know I'm not alone in feeling that I have a personal relationship with Howard and his staff. Their honesty on the air makes me feel like a fly on the wall in a room where they are hanging out bullshitting. I almost feel that I'm not supposed to be listening to the conversation, but it's really fun and really funny.

*"I think when you listen to me, you're an insider. You're in the club. We're not the guy in Roosevelt High School being goofed on when we're all together. We're strong. We're together. Some of us are misfits. Some of us are outcasts. And we can admit our insecurities and we can laugh about them and have a great time,"*
- Howard Stern on *60 Minutes* 12/2005

It doesn't take long for dedicated listeners to get a sense of the different people involved in the show. On what other show do regular listeners or viewers know the majority of the writers, producers, researchers, and interns?

Not only do we know the characters but, in many cases, we know about their relationships and private lives. This insight provides a completely different perspective.

That kind of perspective has allowed *The Howard Stern Show* to expand its brand into other shows like *The Wrap–Up Show*, *The Intern Show*, and *The Superfan Roundtable*. These exist because they take the notion that everything is fair game, and they extend the transparency of *The Howard Stern Show* after Howard has left the building.

This is the foundation of the business genius that is Howard Stern. He understood that people would be interested in the daily ins and outs of creating a radio show and that people would connect with an honest show. America connected with *The Howard Stern Show* to the tune of an estimated fifteen million listeners during its run on traditional radio and access to more than twenty million paid subscribers with the move to satellite radio.

## Anything Goes, I'm an Open Story

Regular *The Howard Stern Show* listeners have the feeling they know Howard personally. His honesty builds trust with his listeners. It allows us to feel that Howard is "one of us" and this bond is further strengthened by the fact that he always presents an authenticity that is indisputable.

You rarely hear people bash their bosses in a

public forum, but if Howard has censorship issues or is in a contract dispute, he pulls no punches.

People are often so uncomfortable with flaws in their appearance that they bury them deep inside, yet there is Howard publicly lamenting the size of his penis (too small) or his nose (too big).

He has made it his mission to educate me on the best, most productive bathroom rituals, right down to how to wipe my ass and what to wipe it with. He has built his reputation and a huge media empire on that kind of honesty.

## Show Your Customers that You're Real

When establishing yourself or your company online, your authenticity will come through quickly. If you're doing shameless self-promotion, people are going to tune you out faster than Howard can talk a stripper out of her clothes.

Be yourself. People prefer to do business with other people, not with robots who sound as if they just completed a course of business buzz words.

Your authenticity is going to come through

much more clearly if you are passionate about what you do. If you drudge through the day, waiting for the clock to strike five, the odds are that even if you are honest, you're not going to inspire anyone to buy your product or do business with your company.

If the inspiration isn't there, move on. There are other options. Moving on can mean finding a new job or refocusing the resources in your current business. If inspiration and passion aren't behind what you do, you're going to appear inauthentic. People don't buy shit from people who don't appear to be honest.

## Call It Like You See It

There's rarely any confusion about where Howard stands on a particular issue. He cuts to the core of his feelings on a topic quickly. We feel comfortable that we know where he stands, and he gives us the opportunity to agree or disagree.

Whether you are a CEO or part of the overnight cleaning crew, your success depends on your ability to assess situations realistically. If you let others do this for you (or worse, trick yourself into believing something about your company or your situation that isn't true), you're not long for this world.

Far too many companies, particularly smaller ones, don't put business performance measurements in place to establish the effectiveness of their teams. Metrics are vital not only for the companies to understand where their workers stand but also for workers to better understand how they are performing and what they can do to improve.

Build a set of measurements that will help you judge success, particularly if none have been provided. Talk to the people that you interact with every day, and learn what they expect from you in terms of tangible results.

Once you know how others keep score, build a scorecard and periodically assess yourself against the criteria you have collected. Look at the data objectively, and make adjustments to improve. Numbers don't lie. They indicate whether or not you've made an honest assessment of yourself and your environment.

On terrestrial radio, Howard was singularly focused on metrics, and the only metric that mattered to him was ratings. If people were listening to his show, he could tell everyone else to go to hell. If advertisers or station management didn't like what he was doing, as long as the listeners were there, he could afford to stick to his approach because listeners meant advertising sales.

## Be Realistic

Give your business a long, hard look. Evaluate your marketplace and your position within the marketplace. Develop a fair assessment of your company's strengths and weaknesses. It cannot be a great company if you overlook your weaknesses.

Develop people with a keen sense for identifying weaknesses, and build a culture that rewards them for speaking up. When weaknesses are identified, tackle them head on.

There is no reward for tiptoeing around issues. More often than not, your company's biggest problems are the "eight-hundred-pound gorilla in the room." Everyone knows they are there and will breathe a sigh of relief when the issues are made public.

## Repeat after Me: "I Am Stupid"

If you are not performing up to expectations on *The Howard Stern Show*, you will likely be called out to defend yourself. To the delight of listeners, many times staffers are called out on the air when they screw up. There have been many times when Scott, the engineer, has been called out for technical difficulties.

It's not always easy, and it is seldom comfortable when you must tell people that they are screwing up at their job. It needs to be done so that the company can grow.

It seems like it is not so easy for Howard to call people out, and I suspect that's why it is so often done over the air. When he addresses business issues during the show, he can hide under the umbrella of "entertainment" to get his point across. There have been some hilarious moments where he insisted that a staff member repeat a mantra to get a point across. These spontaneous, on-air discussions help him avoid the tension of one-to-one communication and criticism.

In the real world, it's not easy to find cover in difficult conversations, but there are ways to make the conversations easier to initiate and more likely to achieve the desired results.

## Identify the End Game

Prepare for your conversation with the desired outcome in mind. If you're confronting someone for a shortcoming, figure out how, in a perfect world, that shortcoming would be overcome. Help people to understand the issues, and work with them to develop solutions.

## Focus on the Job, not the Person

Jobs are about completing tasks to reach a desired outcome. When working to solve performance problems, stay focused on the tasks that are not completed. Explain how the tasks fit into the big picture, and don't make it about the person. Adopt the *Godfather* philosophy. In the film *The Godfather*, Michael Corleone said, "It's not personal, Sonny, it's strictly business." Be prepared for debate, but remain calm and steer the conversation objectively.

## This Is *Not* the Regis and Kathy Lee Show

Howard has interviewed everyone from presidential hopefuls to drunken dwarfs, one interview more compelling than the next. Here are some of the great celebrities we've heard interviewed on *The Howard Stern Show*.

- Arnold Schwarzenegger

- Billy Joel
- Bob Hope
- Paul McCartney
- Chevy Chase
- Christine Todd Whitman
- David Letterman
- Donald Trump
- Farrah Fawcett
- Jennifer Aniston
- Jerry Seinfeld
- O. J. Simpson
- Robert Duvall
- Wilt Chamberlain

One thread ties these interviews together: Howard asked for, even demanded, honesty.

His guests are rarely judged on their success or fame in the entertainment world. He and his fans tend to judge the interview based on how much people are willing to share about themselves. Canned, press-tour answers don't fly on *The Howard Stern Show*. Guests must be prepared to answer questions about themselves that are not included in a press bio.

Most guests know that Howard is going to ask them tough questions that require honest responses. Guest who embrace the questions and share insights not heard elsewhere are wildly popular.

The bottom line for fans is that regardless of why people are famous, if they are open and let Howard guide the interview, they will likely come off as interesting and cool.

On the other end of the spectrum, we find guests who dodge the tough questions. The most popular celebrities in the world look bad if they come into Howard's studio with no knowledge of the show and no clue about what is expected. If they expect a cushy "Regis and Kathy Lee" interview, they're in for shock.

In 2011, a fan called the show and asked Howard who was the biggest "train wreck" he'd ever interviewed. Howard mentioned Warren Beatty, who was a guest on the show in 1988. Howard said on the air, "He's a seriously weird guy, I mean, maybe my skills as an interviewer are better now but I have to think that—I was trying to have a reasonable conversation with him, and he's just a very slow talker and barely says anything."

It's no secret that Warren Beatty's career in Hollywood is marked by stories of being a huge playboy who has been with hundreds of the most beautiful women in Tinsel Town. Did Beatty really believe that he would be able to avoid questions about his sexual conquests on a show where sex stories take center stage? Howard tried to take the conversation there, but Beatty wouldn't open up and be honest.

Howard's frustration came through while he was answering the listeners question about his worst interview:

> *"Talking about pussy is impossible, but he's dedicated his entire life to pussy and the pursuit of it. His whole life is pussy, but he tries to act like he's above it. But it really was the definition of his life, that, and making films. And that's what I wanted to talk about."*
> - Howard Stern, *The Howard Stern Show*, 5/2011

The ultimate irony surrounding the Beatty interview was that the movie he was promoting, "Bulworth," was about a politician who connected with voters only after he had the freedom to say whatever he wanted in an honest or sometimes offensive manner. I guess Beatty didn't learn the lessons from the movie.

## Weave Honesty into Your Corporate Culture

The definitive book about honesty in the

workplace, *Absolute Honesty*, lays out six laws of honesty that every company should integrate into its culture and everything it does.

## 1. Tell the Truth.

It may sound stupid, but telling the truth is a top-down corporate value. If management focuses on sharing news and information with employees, it breeds a culture where honesty is accepted.

When management teams keep secrets from the staff or project teams don't share among themselves, it breeds a culture of uneasiness and destroys trust.

## 2. Tackle the Problem.

Because many corporations are not always open to honest disagreement, people agree with each other for the sake of not "ruffling feathers." That approach nearly always fails to address a company's biggest issues.

Issues remain under the surface, and they grow and grow. People know that they are there, but they don't feel comfortable speaking up. This means the slow death of the organization.

Dialog between employees and leaders needs to be open so that people aren't afraid to expose issues and tackle them.

### 3. Disagree and Commit.

The first two rules push people to communicate honestly with each other and to be brave enough to unearth problems. The third rule is about a new approach to solving problems.

Too often, the people who are focused on solving an issue walk into a room and later emerge with a plan that was hatched by the most vocal people in the room. Outwardly, everyone appears to agree on the direction.

Once the meeting is over, splintered water cooler conversations ensue. People talk about how their ideas were flatly rejected or that the proposed plan is stupid and doomed for failure.

The idea behind "disagree and commit" is to provide everyone the opportunity to speak up. It allows participants to get their thoughts and objections on the table.

The idea is to fight hard for what you believe in and then work to make the solution the best it can be. Once a decision has been made, your job is to commit to the decision and execute on the plan to the best of your ability. It's your job, just f'ing do it!

## 4. Welcome the Truth.

Sometimes, this idea is harder to swallow than a three-foot kielbasa. It is human nature to become defensive when receiving criticism, even when it's delivered the right way.

Although it is difficult, train yourself (and your staff) to share the truth with one another and accept that truth hurts. Those difficult truths are often the most insightful, and they help employees make the biggest strides toward becoming better people and employees.

As mentioned earlier, many organizations use personality profiling to determine how people on a team are most comfortable giving and receiving information. If you decide to conduct personality profiling, consider sharing the results with team members. If your team is in support of sharing, it helps members to understand one another on another level and can help people more effectively work together. To welcome the truth, learn how best to deliver the truth to people based on their personality, and train yourself to be open to discussion about your own job performance.

## 5. Reward the Messenger.

Being honest with your team is hard enough. Getting intentionally or unintentionally screwed to the wall for telling the truth really sucks. Not only does it suck for the people who stick their neck out to be honest about a problem or an issue, but it sucks for the rest of the employees. No one wants to see that being honest and standing by your principals is not valued or, even worse, may irreparably damage your career.

You can "kill a culture of honesty" if you "kill the messenger." Carefully evaluate difficult situations from many angles, reward new insights no matter how painful they may be, and recognize that even inadvertent dishonesty will negatively affect your entire organization.

## 6. Build a Platform of Integrity.

Creating a culture of honesty does not just happen. It starts at the top, and people learn that honesty is a prized trait when they see it in their leaders. Often a culture of honesty starts with leaders providing formal, written declarations of a commitment to honesty to all employees.

In addition to these formal declarations, your team should see commitment play out in practice as decisions are made. If you lead with honesty, the organization will follow.

## Rule #3 Summary

Being honest with your employees, vendors, and customers is more important than ever. With the abundance of social media and global communication, you can more easily be found out if you're being dishonest, and if people don't trust you, they are less likely to do business with you.

Embrace honesty and criticism as methods for growth and innovation. No company ever created anything great without some level of internal conflict.

Encourage people to say their piece, and foster feedback and communication when making tough decisions. Make it clear that once a decision is made, everyone is expected to rally behind it.

When it comes to honesty, if upper management is going to talk the talk, make sure that it walks the walk. Mixed signals are sure to arouse suspicion.

Honesty is about more than telling the truth. It's about putting a human face on your business. People like to do business with other people, not companies.

Use metrics so that you can be honest with yourself. If something isn't working, fail quickly and try something new.

When working with a team, let the members know what is expected of them and what they are being measured against. It's a lot easier to have a conversation with an employee who is underperforming if you can point to specific criteria that are not being met.


Suggested reading:
Johnson, Larry, and Bob Phillips. *Absolute Honesty: Building a Corporate Culture That Values Straight Talk and Rewards Integrity*. New York: AMACOM, American

Quivers, Robin. *Quivers a Life*. NY, NY: HarperCollins, 1995.

# Rule #4: Cut Through the Noise: The Art of the Live Read

Howard has helped many companies move from obscurity to being household names. Companies like Dial-a-Mattress were considered synonymous with *The Howard Stern Show*. Anyone who listened to the show during its heyday can likely tell you why you leave the last "S" off when dialing 1-800-MATTRES (you leave off the "S" for savings!).

Early in his career, Howard had a penchant for reading commercials live on his show versus having his advertisers provide pre-recorded commercials to be played during breaks. The "live read" was a tool that Howard used as a point of differentiation from his competitors. His willingness to sit down with potential advertising clients and explain the benefits of advertising on his show allowed the show to take on a different kind of advertiser.

It was important that the show be able to succeed with advertisers that were not traditional radio brands. Many national and better-known regional brands shied away from the show because of its racy content or because they were afraid they might alienate their more puritanical customers. That opened *The Howard Stern Show* to more aggressive local advertisers. These advertisers placed a higher value on Howard's audience than many national brands.

Howard spent time learning about the products he pitched. He learned about their competitive advantage in the marketplace and what made the products different. If it was a product that Howard could use himself, he did.

During his live commercials, he gave the audience honest interpretations of what he had learned about the products. He often provided "back stories" about these brands, giving his audience insight into the companies that they never would have gotten with a traditional, recorded commercial.

When relating these back stories, he often turned the business owners into pseudo-celebrities. This served two purposes. While it gave his audience a more personal connection with the brand, it fed the egos of the business owners. It becomes awfully difficult to pull your ads from *The Howard Stern Show* when people walk up to you in the street and say they know you or your company because of the show. The advertisers were part of *The Howard Stern Show* family and, as such, got the same treatment as everyone else associated with the show.

Howard delivered to his advertisers a significant return on investment for their advertising dollar, despite the fact that they were paying the highest per-minute rate for prime-time ads.

## The Best Stuff on Earth

Howard was a long-time pitch man for Snapple soft drinks. He pitched Snapple with a passion and voracity rarely seen in radio.

The success of the marriage between the Snapple brand and *The Howard Stern Show* has been attributed to Howard's diligence in getting to know the company and its founders.

I think that there was a certain kinship between Howard and the people at Snapple. Both were unlikely New York success stories, both showed the power of "the little guy," and both showed that Jewish kids from New York can make it big.

The founders of Snapple, Hyman Golden, Arnold Greenberg, and Leonard Marsh, started the company in the 1970s and moved it to Howard's home of Long Island. They were New Yorkers through and through, and Howard wanted to see them succeed. In 1994, with no small debt to *The Howard Stern Show*, Snapple's founders sold the company to Quaker Oats for $1.7 billion. It is widely recognized that Howard's live reads played a key role in Snapple's success.

In what turned out to be a huge mistake, upper management at Quaker Oats quickly restructured Snapple's marketing plan and did away with the mainstays of the brand like Wendy "The Snapple Lady" and Howard's live commercials. The split between Howard and Snapple was less than amicable.

After Quaker Oats pulled its advertising from *The Howard Stern Show*, Howard told the story about how the relationship with Snapple began. He described how the founders of Snapple came to the show in a state of desperation. He described how *The Howard Stern Show* would be Snapple's last attempt to build a market for its product.

Snapple was losing money and hoping that a big push on the Stern Show would revitalize the brand. Howard has said that he knew that his fans would support whatever product he asked them to support. He helped his fans draw a connection between Snapple's success and *The Howard Stern Show* remaining on the air. With that connection, fans felt that by supporting Snapple, they were supporting Howard.

Howard described how Arnold Greenberg came to the radio station for meetings and crowed about how Howard was responsible for saving the company.

After Snapple was sold to Quaker Oats, Howard told a story of how he personally reached out the head of Quaker Oats after its decision to pull Snapple advertising from *The Howard Stern Show*. He suggested that Quaker Oats might reconsider this decision.

As I read between the lines, it seemed like Howard even mentioned to the management team at Quaker Oats that if they pulled advertising, he may propose that his fans boycott the product. After Howard's relationship with Snapple ended, he made his position on Snapple clear: the fan base no longer needed to support the product. Howard didn't phrase it in politically correct terms; he said something like "F-- Snapple!"

## Keep Your Fans Off Balance: Mix Advertising and Content

Howard's commercials are compelling because when you're listening to the show, the line between where the show ends and the commercials begin is blurry. In Howard's days on terrestrial radio, commercials popped up in the middle of an outrageous bit where you could barely understand what the commercial was about because of the laughing and joking.

The advertising airwaves are cluttered like never before. There are hundreds of cable television channels, terrestrial and satellite radio, and Internet platforms including video, social media, podcasts, and Pandora. We see advertising tacked on to everything from toll gates to young girls bottoms (I don't know what the hell "PINK" is, but it doesn't sound like something I want my daughter wearing on her ass).

Mass media advertising filtering has changed nearly as radically. It used to be that if you didn't want to watch commercials during your favorite television program, you got up to get a beer and take a leak.

With the 1999 introduction of TiVo, that changed. If people were willing to watch their favorite television shows on a slight delay, they no longer needed to sit through commercials. They just hit the fast-forward button, and the commercials whizzed by with all but their most elemental branding lost.

Advertisers developed new and creative ways to respond to these new tools. With product placement, many savvy companies integrated their advertising into the consumer content.

The result is a strange animal that is part entertainment and part advertisement. It's blatant and becoming more commonplace.

Whether we see BMW's latest model in a feature film or red Coca-Cola glasses prominently displayed on the *American Idol* judges' table, product placement has gone mainstream. *Business Week* reported in 2008 that *American Idol* had more than five hundred and eighty product placements. That's a lot of gratuitous Coke cup shots and Ford-sponsored commercials.

Product placement is showing up in places that many "purists" consider off limits to paid promotion. In July, 2008 *The New York Times* reported that product placement was finding its way into television news casts. Fox5 affiliate KVVU in Las Vegas was paid by McDonald's to have its iced coffee set in front of news anchors. For many people, the idea of news shows using product placement to make a buck is disconcerting. What if a newscast included a story on how McDonald's food was really, really bad for you? Could this influence the tone of the story?

The trend of mingling content audiences are interested in with advertising will grow. The people who are best at it and those who have the most strategic partnerships will be in a better position to flourish than those who don't get on the bus.

## I Can't Afford Product Placement on *American Idol*!

Traditional media is not the only place that product promotion is intricately and purposefully weaved into consumable content. Social media websites are a favorite target for marketers who promote a brand by cloaking an advertisement in the veil of entertainment.

This type of marketing is often referred to as "viral" or "conversational" marketing. When effectively executed, it can be an extremely powerful and cost-effective means of promotion.

Many of the most widely read blogs on the Internet feature posts that include affiliate links to products. (Affiliate programs are revenue-sharing programs set up by product and service companies.) In these programs, the advertiser (the company selling the product) sets up an arrangement with the publisher (the company promoting the product). When the publisher sends traffic to the advertiser's site and that traffic results in a sale, the publisher is entitled to a commission on that sale.

Affiliate programs can be very lucrative, and sites that have significant traffic can make a lot of money by sending consumers to purchase the products of other companies. There is nothing unethical or illegal about creating affiliate links within your content, but in 2009, the FCC updated its guidelines about deceptive advertising. Under the guidelines, anyone who is being paid to write about a product, or anyone who will get paid as a result of driving traffic to another website, must disclose this to the site visitors. For more information about disclosing affiliate relationships, visit business.ftc.gov.

## Where Is Your Superfan Roundtable?

Using his two stations on Sirius Satellite radio, Howard developed new shows with *The Howard Stern Show* as the premise. In one spinoff, the *Superfan Roundtable*, the fans are invited to come in and discuss elements of the show.

Occasionally, Howard's celebrity fans get together for the *Celebrity Superfan Roundtable*. These roundtables have included David Arquette, Howie Mandel, and Jeff Probst from the TV show *Survivor*.

If you are a product or service company, the odds are that someone is writing about your product or service. There are likely blogs, Facebook pages, and Twitter accounts dedicated to your product or service.

Seek out these blogs and social media outlets and begin connecting with the people who visit and contribute to these sites (google.com/blogsearch is a great place to start).

Once you have found the websites that are relevant to your industry and identified blog owners and top contributors, design a plan to connect with these people. Build a compelling case as to why they should write about or review your product. Explain the benefits to the blogger as well as to his or her audience.

It's important to connect with these people on a personal level. Spamming hundreds of writers and hoping for a response will not yield any valid results and may create negative attention. If a site has readers, and you have an offering that fits the theme of the blog and its audience, you have a starting point.

When you run across bloggers who are fans of your product, you have an opportunity to expand the relationship to longer-term, win-win partnerships. Affiliate programs are often a great place to start.

If you have a product that lends itself to affiliate marketing, establish an affiliate program. Affiliate programs help blogs monetize traffic (earn money from having a lot of website visitors) and readership. It never hurts to dangle dollar signs in front of bloggers. Many blog owners struggle to profit from their blog and are looking for new opportunities to monetize their traffic.

When it comes to creating an affiliate program, there are literally thousands of firms that can help you get started. Be sure that the company is well established and that its core values match those of your company. To learn more about affiliate marketing and networks, performinsider.com is a great resource.

Understanding affiliate marketing and getting involved in the affiliate marketing community provides value far beyond affiliate marketing itself. Affiliate marketers tend to be on the cutting edge of everything related to Internet marketing, and they are the first to test and prove new marketing approaches.

Keep your finger on the pulse of the affiliate marketing community, and you will be a better marketer.

## Outbound versus Inbound Marketing

If marketing messages are filtered by consumers like never before, what else can a company do to get its message heard by the right prospects? Over the last few years, there has been a groundswell of *inbound marketing* versus traditional *outbound marketing*.

Traditional outbound marketing is about blasting your message to a broad audience. You do your research and profile the people or companies that are most likely to buy your products. You gather the demographic information of your target customers and identify the media where your targets are most likely to hear your message. Outbound marketers know that even with the best research and perfect execution, only a small percentage of people who come across your message are actually prospects, a smaller percentage will see your message, and an even smaller percentage will take action.

# Inbound Part I: When Your Customers Are Looking for You, Be There

Inbound marketing shifts your marketing efforts towards prospects who are seeking your product or service. It focuses on people who want to take action because they have a "pain point" or a desire.

While traditional marketing often focuses on creating a need, inbound marketing focuses on being front and center when a need arises and your prospects search for solutions.

The first step in the inbound marketing process is getting found. The idea of "getting found" is at the heart of the $35 billion of advertising revenue that Google generated in 2011.

Through Google's Adwords tool, advertisers display ads on Google's search results based on the specific words entered into Google's search box. Google helps inbound marketers identify who is searching for their product or service and target them at the moment they are a searching. If a prospect sees your ad and clicks through to your site, you pay Google a "finder's fee."

People who have used Google Adwords know that it can be effective, but it can also become a major expense. That's why so many companies have developed a search engine optimization (SEO) strategy to compliment any paid advertising efforts. SEO helps prospects find you online when they search Google by creating content that Google believes most closely matches what the person is searching for.

SEO is about getting your website to rank high in Google's search results without having to pay Google every time someone clicks through to your website from Google's search results.

Online marketers have found that the more relevant content they have on the web, the more likely Google and other search engines are to include your content in their search results.

This content-creation strategy is why more companies have started to regularly publish new content in the form of blog posts and other valuable free information resources.

When you constantly create new content, you let Google and other search engines know that your website is "fertile soil" for new ideas related to your industry. This helps your site rank higher with more relevant search results.

Keyword-rich posts contain specific words and phrases that customers commonly type into Google when they're looking for products or services. Savvy marketers make sure that their blog posts are rich with keywords.

## Inbound Part II: Once They Find You, Woo Them

As most marketers know, driving traffic to your website is not the end game, it's the first step. Once you have visitors, you need to engage them right away, and continue to provide them with reasons to come back to your site after they visit.

Provide your visitors with offers that they consider valuable.

Make your offers so compelling that to take advantage of the them, your visitors are willing to tell you a little something about themselves.

I'm not talking about a long list of personal contact information, start simple. Usually a valid email address is enough.

## Inbound Part III: Make 'em a Customer

Once you have a prospects email address, you can begin to engage them in a digital conversation. This conversation can take place via email, on the web, using blogs, or through social media sites.

During these conversations your goal is not to be pitching products, your goal is to continue providing value and building trust. Show your prospects that you are a thought leader in your industry, make them care about what you have to say by creating exceptional content.

## Inbound Part IV: Don't Rest

Inbound marketing is a game of continuous improvement. In order to maintain customer loyalty, increase visitor conversion and grow sales, you need to always be testing new customer offers, designing new web pages, and engaging in social networks.

When you keep an eye on what your customers and prospects are saying about you, you can act swiftly to take advantage of positive trends or to minimize the downside of failed efforts.

## The King of Social Media?

Howard and his staff have adopted Twitter as the primary social network to interact with their fans. The Stern Show has no less than 20 twenty active Twitter users, many of which are "verified" users - meaning that Twitter recognizes them for who they say they are (not imposters). Even Howard's bodyguard and driver, Ronnie "The Limo Driver" Munde, is active on Twitter, and his profile is verified.

Shortly after becoming a Twitter user, Howard found a new and creative way to connect with his fans using the platform. On February 12, 2011 at about 4:45 p.m. Howard's movie Private Parts was airing on HBO in New York. He stopped to watch it and decided to start tweeting commentary about the film as it played.

He commented on different scenes, provided insight about to who was on the movie set during certain scenes

(Teri Hatcher), and pointed out elements that were true to life rather than things that were manipulated for the film. It was like a multi-media "pop-up" video event for the movie. People loved it. I believe it was one of the best uses of Twitter for entertainment to date. It was completely unique, and it was completely Howard's idea.

Almost a year later, on New Year's Eve in 2011, Howard once again made celebrity Twitter history. He and his wife, Beth, had a few drinks and decided to call some of Howard's Twitter followers if they provided their phone number. It started with an innocent tweet: "Beth and I are drunk dialing. What's your phone number?" Soon, people were sending Howard their phone numbers and getting phone calls from the King of All Media himself! What a thrill for the fans, and what a way to reinforce your brand as a down- to- earth DJ who is committed to his fans.

## The Facebook Factor

In addition to search engines, marketers are successfully tapping into Facebook to promote their messages to prospects. The 163 million Americans on Facebook spend an average of 15 minutes a day on the site.

People use these sites to stay informed of what's happening in their circle of friends and in the world. They ask their friends for recommendations about what products to buy and who they should work with.

Integrating your company and its message into social platforms is critical. The line between advertising and straight communication is as fuzzy here as it is anywhere. Again, the trick with Facebook is to refrain from spewing self-serving "advertising-speak." Focus on providing content that your prospects find valuable or entertaining. Facebook clearly understands the value of "cutting through the noise" as it continues to weave its advertisers throughout its user generated content.

## Rule #4 Summary

*Stern Show* listeners can often rattle off a long list of advertisers, past and present that used the show to get their message out. They remember because Howard integrated the advertising message into the show. By using live-reads, listeners didn't know where the show ended and the commercials began, and they helped Howard and his advertisers make memorable radio.

When marketing is everywhere, you need to cut through the noise in the marketplace. Consumers are getting better at filtering messages that are not important to them.

Integrate your marketing message into content and you have a great way to get people thinking about your product without the "hard sell."

Millions of people are interested in promoting products and services for a small slice of the sale, and affiliate marketers are interested in promoting your product to their audience. Find the right affiliates, and you've built a global, tech-savvy sales force whose interests align perfectly with your own.

Sending outbound advertising messages takes a big budget and provides lower returns than inbound marketing strategies. Inbound marketing strategies help your prospects find you, engage with you, and ultimately do business with you. Be there when they are looking, and present the message they want to hear. For more on Inbound Marketing, visit Greystack.com.

Social media websites have emerged as required channels for all marketers. Learn how to use Facebook and other social sites to connect with your customers, it's a great way to intertwine content with marketing.

Suggested reading:
Kukral, Jim F. *Attention! This Book Will Make You Money: How to Use Attention-getting Online Marketing to Increase Your Revenue.* Hoboken, NJ: Wiley, 2010.

# Rule #5: Obsessive Passion Is Contagious

Howard's passion for his radio show is indisputable. In fact, some call his love for the show obsessive-compulsive or even neurotic. He has said that when he goes on the air, he loses himself for those three or four hours. He is so passionate about providing his audience with the best radio show and making his team and his guests the best they can be that he often forgets what happens as he moves from segment to segment during the show.

The chapter "It's Your Job, Just F'ing Do It" discussed how hiring enthusiasm is as important, if not more so, than hiring experience. If you are hiring people who are self-motivated and enthusiastic, you will get results from your team regardless of the tasks they are given.

Once you've assembled the right people, they're not going to stay enthusiastic without passionate leadership. For Howard, it's one thing to build a team that's enthusiastic about pulling together the most unique, entertaining radio show in history. It's another to keep that team passionate about getting up at four o'clock in the morning every day.

Keep your team focused on creating a better show today than the one yesterday.

## The Show Above All Else

In sports, it is often said that the most successful teams have a leader that is not only at the top of the game, who would be considered an elite player on any team, but one who is also the hardest-working person in practice and on the field.

Teams with this kind of leadership are successful because everyone on the team recognizes their leader's mastery of the game and, at the same time, recognize that their leader is not satisfied with their success. They know that something bigger drives great players to be even greater. They see that there is work to do and that they must contribute to the greater good. The leader's passion elevates the team, and he leads by example.

*"And maybe that's why I get paid a lot of*

*money. When you hire me, you hire a nut who is going to work 24 hours a day for you and never, ever burn his audience."*
- Howard Stern on *60 Minutes* 12/2005

Throughout his career, Howard has passionately pursued success. He is both a team member and the team leader.

He has long been a creative force during the writing sessions for the show as well as a tireless contributor to the success of projects like his original WWOR *Channel 9* TV show. This tireless passion helped him build and maintain long-term credibility with his teammates.

Great leaders understand that a key component of leadership is leading by example. Leaders show their teams the way by acting in the best interest of the team first and putting their own interests second. I can't think of too many examples where Howard put anything before the best interests of his show.

On September 11, 2001 when New York and other American cities were under attack, Howard put *The Howard Stern Show* first. While speculation rose as to whether the radio station should be evacuated for safety reasons, he continued with the show, reporting from his perspective and in many cases making observations about the situation that others were afraid to make until the situation unfolded. Howard said, "It's war."

Many listeners told me that they gained a new respect for Howard and *The Howard Stern Show* that day.

The most passionate teams are those that have a strong, clear sense of purpose. By providing your team with direction and a practical roadmap for success, you give them the inspiration to achieve. Great leaders identify a long-term vision and help their team to buy into the vision.

## The Spirit of the Law

Howard arrives early at work and stays until the work of the show is completed. This makes it easy for him to hold people like the habitually tardy writer Benjy Bronk accountable when he is late to the studio or not demonstrating the required level of commitment to the show.

Although accountability is never taken lightly, I like that Howard also takes into account the human element and tends to stick to the spirit rather than the letter of the law. In every organization, every team or team member has a specific role with a specific outcome that is defined by a process. The best leaders know the process and its outcome. They are tied one hundred percent not to the process but rather to the result.

Like many great leaders, Howard provides for flexibility within processes as long as the outcomes don't suffer. By applying the spirit of the law, leaders like Howard score big points on the human aspects of work and build incredible loyalty.

## Clear the Way

Howard is a champion for every member of his staff. He seems to do everything he can to ensure that any obstacles to someone getting their job done are obliterated. Many of the on-air discussions about the inner workings of *The Howard Stern Show* are focused on improving work flow and making sure that people can do their jobs without having to jump through hoops.

Take the time to talk with your team members, understand their motivations, and support their needs. It's critical to your success as a leader. Build rock-solid relationships with your team so that everyone understands what will help maintain high levels of passion and performance.

Howard also does a great job of "running interference" for his team when it comes to station management and other "higher ups." He takes much of the heat so that the people doing the work "in the trenches" can get their jobs done without distraction.

## Praise Is Cheap but Valuable

Based on the on-air praise of some of *The Howard Stern Show* staffers, as well as the acknowledgements in his published books, you get the feeling that Howard is better at recognizing staff contributions than he'd admit (although he is also probably tougher on his staff than he'd admit).

The radio industry has a long-standing tradition of crappy pay. Howard likely learned early on that to effectively motivate his team, he needed to heap praise on them when they contributed. It doesn't cost a dime to tell an intern that he or she is doing well or that a writer's contribution to an interview or on-air bit is valuable, but it goes a long way toward job satisfaction.

*"I truly love those people I work with and I appreciate everything they do for me and I just don't say it enough."*
- Howard Stern on *60 Minutes* 12/2005

## Think Beyond Your Reign

In a recent interview in *Rolling Stone*, interviewer Neil Strauss mentioned that Howard's second tour of duty at Sirius Satellite radio may have been inspired by two elements. The first was his ability to grow the Sirius listener base by creating apps for smartphone users that allowed them to listen to the show on their smartphones. The second, and perhaps more powerful, element was his strong desire to craft two talk radio stations into media powerhouses that could outlive him.

By laying out this vision of the future for his staff, Howard showed his staff that they were important to him and that he was working hard to ensure that they had a future. This type of expression of a vision helps teams to pull together in challenging times and emerge victorious.

Howard has effectively instilled a sense of purpose in his team. He has helped to create an emotional connection between his staff and the entity that has become *The Howard Stern Show*.

He has provided his team members with a clear understanding of their roles, how they fit into the big picture, and how every move they make translates to the success of the show.

## Make it Fun

Teams bond through shared experiences and being able to see the human side of each other. At *The Howard Stern Show*, bonding among staff members takes place through informal rivalries as well as through promotions like contests. When the team first got to Satellite radio, they held a contest where each staff member had to reveal a secret that had never before been revealed. During the contest, Howard admitted to having plastic surgery and Robin admitted to having sex with meat and vegetables.

More recently, the team conducted a staff IQ contest where people wagered on whether their IQ was higher than other staffers. The results of that test showed that wack-packer "Wendy the Retard" was at the bottom of the list while segment producer and researcher Will Murray came in at the top, much to the disappointment of many staff hopefuls.

These types of friendly competitions make

work a fun place to be. Do what you can to help your team enjoy the experience of coming to work. Little things are often all it takes to take the edge off in a workplace.

I have always been a huge fan of the four o'clock happy hour—it's hard for people to resist the opportunity to leave work an hour early on a Friday afternoon. When I take people out of the office an hour early and put a drink in their hands, it helps everyone lower their guard and connect. Some issue from the office inevitably comes up during conversation and more often than not is resolved there at the bar.

Adding toys and games to break areas has been a popular way to help employees interact with one another since the first wave of Internet companies started in the late 1990s. If you have room for a ping-pong table, go for it!

Center some fun events around lunch. Potluck lunches around a theme can create a party atmosphere and a lot of laughs. Have people cook a Mexican feast for Cinco de Mayo or Cajun food for Mardi Gras. You never know when a party might break out!

Allow freedom of expression by holding an office/cubicle decorating day. Those old "inspirational" posters are, well, old. Decorate your walls with bright paint and interesting, fun posters. For many years, Howard decorated the back of his studio door with naked pictures of his fans and listeners. Find a fun theme for decorating the common spaces in your office, and get everyone to contribute.

When scheduling events to make things fun with your coworkers, do them during, immediately prior, or after the work day. Events outside of work hours and forcing people to make a special trip severely affects the turn out, and people feel pressured to attend, making it not so fun after all.

Take the time from within the workday. You might lose a few hours of productivity, but the time will be made back in the long term as you create a happy, motivated, engaged team.

## Rule #5 Summary

Without passion, your business is doomed. Howard's maniacal passion to bring his listeners the greatest radio show in history is a cornerstone of his success.

Bringing the right people into your organization is the first step, and keeping them engaged and passionate is the key to long-term success. Give your people the authority to make tough decisions and the freedom to explore new ideas. If Howard's staff members feared being fired for coming up with outlandish ideas, many of the show's most memorable moments may have never happened.

Champion your staff members and protect them. In any size of organization, provide "air cover" for your staff members. If they get flak from other areas of the company, deflect it toward yourself so that your staff members can continue their work.

It doesn't cost a thing to tell people that they are doing a great job, and although it can feel a little cheesy, it is appreciated more than you would think. People enjoy a pat on the back.

Make decisions for the long term, and communicate your strategies to your staff. When you let them know why you're doing something, they may not always agree with you, but they will at least know the end game.

Work is a necessary evil for most people, so do what you can to make coming to work rewarding and fun. Do something fun for fun's sake. Time spent having fun isn't necessarily productive, but it will amp up the productivity when people return to work.

Suggested reading:
Linkner, Josh. *Disciplined Dreaming: A Proven System to Drive Breakthrough Creativity*. San

Francisco: Jossey-Bass, 2011.

Vaynerchuk, Gary. *Crush It!: Why Now Is the Time to Cash in on Your Passion.* [New York]: HarperStudio, 2009.

Yerkes, Leslie. *Fun Works: Creating Places Where People Love to Work.* San Francisco: Berrett-Koehler, 2001.

# Rule #6:
# Have the Loyalty of an English Bulldog

Few celebrities can boast that they have a fan base as loyal or committed as Howard's. There are many times where he has asked his fans to support him in a cause, and they always seem to rise to the occasion.

Some of the more influential moves he and his fans take at least partial credit for are politically based. Few would dispute that Howard played an important role in the election of New York Governor George Pataki and New Jersey Governor Christine Todd Whitman.

Pataki had Howard on the podium during his swearing-in ceremony, and Governor Whitman named a highway rest stop in New Jersey after Howard in recognition of his support.

Howard's fan loyalty is in large part a result of his unwavering loyalty to them. He always puts his fans first.

On terrestrial radio, Howard's focus was on spreading the show across the country and being the number one show in every market he entered. He knew that he couldn't do it himself. He enlisted people in these markets to help spread the word about the show.

When entering new markets, early adopters of the show and displaced fans helped *The Howard Stern Show* "go viral" before anyone heard the term. Building a small but intense legion of fans in a city gave Howard a foothold that he could build upon to grow the base.

I was already a long-time Howard show listener in the New York market when I left for college in Albany, New York. Albany is about three hours north of New York, and it is also a completely different media market.

Going from New York to Albany was an interesting experience. The local nightly news shows struck me first. They were obviously less polished and the anchors much less charismatic than those in NYC.

Beyond the local news, the commercials seemed like an endless stream of local car dealers screaming at the camera, and the radio shows were largely of the "morning zoo" variety—lame jokes and a cast of largely uninteresting characters laughing at each other.

No one in the Capital District was happier than me when it was announced that Howard was coming to Albany on rock station Q-104, WQBK FM in 1992. I was finally free of the dopey *Mason and Sheehan Show,* the local morning show that Albany locals considered irreverent and funny. Those of us who knew better sat back and waited for the Stern hurricane to arrive.

I began listening to Howard's show the first day it aired, and slowly but surely people began to catch on. I pushed friends and coworkers who listened to the "wannabe" morning show to tune into "the real deal."

We were the army, spreading the word about *The Howard Stern Show*. When Howard began to aggressively syndicate the show, he proudly pumped up the new cities that he brought on board. He ranted about local station managers who were not abiding by the syndication rules, and he aggressively attacked the incumbent morning shows. As new cities came on board, he incorporated them into the show to make his new listeners feel like they were in on the joke.

There was definitely a formula: Move into a market, and pick a fight with the biggest, most popular, incumbent morning show. Start a battle that will get you huge local exposure, and build a legion of fans by providing them with the best entertainment in morning radio. Once you take over the number one spot, declare victory, celebrate with your fans, and move on to the next city. Howard used the formula to spread like a virus across the country from New York to Los Angeles.

## Celebrate the Successes

One of the keys to Howard's syndication success formula was celebrating with his fans once they helped him reach number one in a market. The practice of giving back to your customers once they help you reach a milestone has been around forever, and Howard employed it perfectly.

Howard's fan celebrations are legendary. He held "funerals" for the morning radio show disc jockeys that he beat in the ratings from Philadelphia to Los Angeles and a host of cities in between.

These events were attended by huge crowds of fans who wanted to be a part of the celebration and to get a glimpse of the King of All Media.

In Los Angeles, Howard dressed as a Roman

emperor and guillotined competing DJs Mark and Brian in effigy.

In Cleveland, he took WNCX from number thirteen to number one in the Cleveland morning radio ratings in less than two years. In June 1994, while doing his "funeral" for the local morning programs on WMJI and WMMS, Howard dressed as a military leader to signify "D-Day" for his competition. The Cleveland "funeral" turned into more of a war than even Howard was expecting. During the broadcast, William Alford, an engineer from competing station WMMS, cut the cable that uplinked Howard's show to the satellite. Howard recovered by continuing the show over phone wires, and the show went down as a classic in Stern show history.

As the story of the cut wire unfolded, Howard was adamant about public pursuit and prosecution of the Alford, and in 1995, Alford was sentenced to ten days in prison and a fine.

Celebrating your success with your supporters is not a new concept. Some people remember the days where department stores threw a party and heaped huge rewards on an unsuspecting individual for being the one millionth customer. That was giving back to the community and to the customer base.

Today, it is easier to reward your entire customer base, not just one lucky person who through sheer luck stumbles through the door at the right moment.

When your company conducts business online, you develop a database of customer names, addresses, and email addresses. Stay connected with these customers.

Don't confuse the idea of staying connected with your customers with constantly spamming them with sales offers. Offer them exclusive deals that only previous customers can get. Make them feel special for doing business with you time and time again.

When you make them feel special and commit to their needs, you can ask things of them that other companies cannot.

What company other than Apple could ask customers to wait in a line for two days to get their hands on a new cellphone? Apple makes its customers feel special, like they are part of a club. They talk to each other in their own language and seem to have a kinship simply because they share a love for Apple products.

## Ideas with Handles

Howard's fans do things that no other fans in the world do. It's not just limited to our inbred reaction to scream Baba Booey! Stern Rules! Howard Stern's Penis! when we are within earshot of any mass media. We are creative thinkers and we dream up things to promote Howard that other celebrity fans don't.

*The Howard Stern Show* gives listeners what Chris Brogan and Julien Smith, the authors of *Trust Agents*, call "ideas with handles." When we listen to *The Howard Stern Show* and hear clips of other listeners making phony phone calls or screaming Howard's name to get media attention or writing funny parodies about Robin's big, beautiful breasts, we are more than just amused. Many listeners hear these messages and think, "I would have done it *this* way." We think about what would have made it funnier for *us*. This is an example of how *The Howard Stern Show* "soldiers" take ideas from the show and create new uses or variations of a theme.

How does this relate to business? According to Brogan and Smith, it might mean holding periodic meetings to brainstorm the shared vision of a product or service. It means sharing external ideas from books and the web that are in line with the team's plans or goals. By sharing this information with your team, you create an internal dialog and provoke ideas that might not otherwise come to light.

In some sense, this is the foundation of using social media at your company. Using social media platforms to share ideas among employees and to start conversations about products and services can help a company hash out a strategy or vision much quicker than with a series of meetings with a few participants.

A great example of how Howard mobilizes his loyal fan base came in early 2007 when he called upon his fans to help derail the hottest show on television, *American Idol.*

Howard had a guy named Dave Della Terza on his show. Della Terza created a website, votefortheworst.com, dedicated "to support voting for the entertaining contestants who the producers would hate to see win on *American Idol.*"

Howard took the concept to a whole new level. He strongly encouraged his audience to vote for the site's favorite contestant, Sanjaya Malakar. Sanjaya seemed like nice enough but was clearly less talented than some of the other contestants. The show's star judge at the time,

Simon Cowell, claimed that if Sanjaya won he would not return to the show as a judge.

Howard was able to mobilize his legions of fans and got them to vote for Sanjaya week after week. Stern Superfan Jeff the Drunk claimed to have voted for Sanjaya more than 300 times. Sanjaya lasted through week seven of the show, which guaranteed him a spot on the Idol tour, and this was in large part due to *The Howard Stern Show*.

## If You Have Loyal Fans, You Have Options

Howard must know that guys like me who have been faithful listeners for many years have woven the show into the fabric of their lives and that it's not easy to stop listening. It would be like losing an old friend.

He put his fans' loyalty to the test, and he put his money where his mouth was, in 2004 when he announced that he was leaving the terrestrial radio airwaves and heading to satellite radio. He did not know how his fans would react, but he must have felt that he needed to change his show in order to be true to himself and his vision for the show. Howard made it clear through the radio show that he was finding it increasingly difficult to deliver a great show in the face of censorship pressures from radio station management, the FCC, and privately sponsored censorship groups.

He asked his fans to start paying to continue listening to *The Howard Stern Show*.

At the time, there were only about a million subscribers to Sirius Satellite radio, and the company needed a significant boost in subscribers if it was going to survive, let alone compete and win against its larger competitor, XM Radio.

By the time Howard hot the satellite airwaves for his first broadcast in January 2006, he had already exceeded subscriber targets set by Sirius in its deal, and he and his super-agent, Don Buchwald, received a reported thirty-four million shares of Sirius stock as a result.

The stock was part of an incentive plan that Howard agreed to, based on subscriber growth at Sirius. About a year later, Howard received another twenty-two million shares of stock based on the increase of subscribers in 2006. It was reported that the Sirius subscriber based in the United States at the end of 2006 was about six million. This exceeded Sirius' targets by more than two million listeners.

Howard made the transition from terrestrial

radio to satellite, made significantly more money, while bringing along his most loyal fans. He proved that he was worth paying for.

## Loyal Fans Will Pay for the Upgrade

Build a loyal customer base by providing an exceptional product, and you can ask customers to do things other companies may not be able to.

In the software and service industries, more companies are incorporating "freemium" offerings into their mix. Freemium models are those where a base (a scaled-back version of a product or service) is given to customers at no charge. Customers have the option to pay "up-charges" to add features or increase their usage of the product or service.

If you provide a great core product, people will pay for the upgrade. It's up to you to creatively give your prospects a free taste of what you have to offer so that they later become paying customers.

The company Dropbox used the freemium model to become the most popular cloud-based storage company on the web.

If you're unfamiliar with the company,

Dropbox allows you do add a storage folder to your computer that looks and feels like any other folder. When you save a file to your Dropbox folder, a copy is stored on Dropbox's servers on the Internet or "in the cloud." The stored files are accessible to you from any Internet-connected device with the Dropbox software.

I use Dropbox to share files across my iPhone, my Dell Laptop, my Mac desktop, and the media center connected to the television in my living room.

Dropbox provides 2 gigabytes (GB) of storage for free. Its service is so convenient and simple to use that most users fall in love with it and upgrade to a paid version that allows them to store more data.

It was rumored that Apple tried to acquire Dropbox in 2009, but the founders rejected the offer. With more than fifty million users, a round of venture funding that values the company at $4 billion, and a freemium model to die for, it seems like Dropbox made the right choice.

A variation of the freemium model is the free-to-pay conversion model. Companies that employ this model provide a fully functional service for free. They build a huge customer base, ensure that their customers have integrated their product into their lifestyle, and then change the rules. They charge a small fee to all their users, employ a freemium model where features that were previously free now have a cost, or they expose their customers to new content such as advertising.

Facebook and Twitter both shifted gears once they developed a following. Facebook's founder, Mark Zuckerberg, kept advertisers off the site for as long as he could because advertising "wasn't cool" and could slow the growth of Facebook. Once Facebook grew, advertising was slowly integrated into the site, and the company began making truckloads of money.

## Put Your Money Where Your Mouth Is

If you have the luxury of negotiating your own compensation plan, consider incorporating performance bonuses as part of the deal. It used to be that only sales people could be paid based on their job performance—they received sales commissions. Today, particularly with the ability to measure results using technology, there are many ways to track customer activities and sources of revenue.

If you can link your compensation to measurable benefits that you bring to your company, do so. This provides people in an organization with a compensation "ceiling" the opportunity to make more than the average by risking some guaranteed salary.

Ensure that the terms of your pay-for-performance benefits are laid out with little room for interpretation.

Take a lesson from Howard and his battles with Sirius over subscriber-level bonuses. He built into his contract certain bonus levels based on the number of people who subscribed to Sirius radio.

When Sirius acquired XM Radio, Howard felt that the subscribers who came along with the acquisition should be included when calculating subscriber-based bonuses. Howard filed a suit to collect based on the combined subscribership of the company.

SiriusXM radio disagreed, and in 2012, a federal court dismissed the suit. Howard appealed the decision, and we'll have to wait to see how it shakes out.

## Reap What You Sow

Provide value to your audience without expecting anything in return. If you are constantly selling, you are not providing value to people who are not yet your customers. You need to give your prospects value prior to adding them as customers.

Howard built his fan base on radio, a free platform, and did not try to convert those listeners to customers until after he established his value to those fans. He built an audience and only then asked them to become "customers." Once he had their faith, he never shied away from making money from his fans.

He unabashedly asked fans to support advertisers, to support various television programs, and to pay to watch pay-per-view *HowardTV*. He made millions on his audio box set, *Crucified by the FCC*, and an alleged $23 million on his video *Butt-Bongo Fiesta* and his New Year's Eve pay-per-view special. He asked his listeners to support him as "America's Judge" on the TV show *America's Got Talent*.

Every one of these events was extensively promoted on the radio show.

He doesn't exploit his audience for money. He doesn't sell merchandise, t-shirts, coffee mugs, mouse pads, or any of that crap. He focuses on providing his fans a great experience for free with the radio show and then makes sure that great experience carries through to any products he asks them to purchase.

How do you lay similar groundwork in your business? Provide value to your prospect *before* asking them to buy.

Let's say that you are a real estate agent focused on helping buyers find new homes. Providing people the best, most complete information on properties for sale in their areas of interest is huge. In addition to providing the best photos and descriptions of the homes, you need to supplement that information with great community information. Let them know where to take their kids on weekends and for celebrations, where to walk their dogs to meet like-minded dog owners, and where to take their dry cleaning if they want to support green, earth-friendly cleaning methods.

In addition to the "soft information," do some market analysis based on the transactions in your town. Tell potential buyers and sellers what types of houses are selling. What is the average price per square foot in the marketplace? How does the house they are looking at stack up against the mean? What are the other considerations if a given house falls above or below the average? What are the pricing trends in the marketplace? Are prices rising sharply or sinking to new lows?

Give your prospects a complete picture of their situation, and give them that information for free. They will remember you as the local expert, and when they are ready to make a move, you'll be the one they call.

The communication platforms today allow you to stay connected with your friends and audience in ways previously unheard of. The connections you make remind people that you are there and a valuable resource. Perhaps more importantly, it helps them to remember you.

When they come across an opportunity that fits your business, the contacts that you've made via email, Twitter, and Facebook will come to you instead of a competitor.

## Remaining an Insider Can Be Just as Important as the Product

I sat down for Howard's 1994 New Year's Eve Pay-per-View TV special with great anticipation. I had invited six or so buddies to come over to watch Howard's *New Year's Rotten Eve*. As soon as Howard popped up through the stage (while sitting on a toilet during the opening number), I had a sense that this show might be over the top. Howard was well suited for radio and the stream-of-conscious discussion that came with it. It had been my experience that Howard didn't translate well to TV where dialogue was more tightly scripted.

I considered the special okay at best. There were some funny highlights to discuss with the boys as we headed out to enjoy the remainder of 1994.

Even though I may have been unhappy with the special, I was still glad that I paid my money to see it. When the radio show came back on the air after the holidays and all the talk was about what happened on New Year's Eve, I was still on the inside when the stories. I knew the context of everything that Howard and his team were talking about. I started to think that maybe I had missed something, because the fans calling in thought the show was unbelievably great!

My loyalty to the show did not waiver. Even if I was not very entertained by the $25 special, I remained an insider, and knew what everyone was talking about afterward.

I think about all those people who stood in line to get their hands on Apple's latest iPhone.

There is no doubt that many of them were disappointed that they weren't getting certain features that exist in other competing phones. But they did it so that they could be the first to have it and could be "on the inside" of conversations about it.

Like Howard, Apple has an uncanny way of making you feel like an insider when you purchase its products. When you feel like an insider, you will pay a premium and repay the company with loyalty even if, in some cases, it is blind loyalty.

## Great Customer Service Means Loyalty

The loyalty that Howard shows to his fans can easily translate to the customer service that companies give their customers. A customer's loyalty to a brand is often just as centered on a company's attitude and customer-service philosophy as it is on its products.

In the retail space, it is often the case that you have the same products as hundreds or thousands of other retailers in the country. If you are a shoe store, the odds are that the shoes you sell to people who walk through your door are the same ones they can find in two or three other stores close by. Your Versace shoes are the same as theirs, and your Nike Shox are identical to their Nike Shox.

Once you realize this, determine what you can do to make people buy *your* Versace shoes instead of theirs.

You can discount your shoes more than the store down the street and compete on price, hoping to capture the bargain shoppers, or you could invest in customer service. You might invest in training a knowledgeable sales staff that really knows the shoes and how to interact with customers. You might invest in nice, comfortable chairs for your customers to sit in when trying on their shoes. You might even invest in a customer-loyalty program and provide discounts to regular customers. These are all good strategies.

You're not likely to start taking shoes back after people have left the store and worn them for a few days, a week, or a month. What if they just bought those Versace shoes to wear to their sister's wedding and now they want to return them? What are they crazy?

Enter Zappos. Most would consider Zappos an online shoe company, but it considers itself a *customer service* company. What's the difference?

It offers free shipping both ways on all its

shoes, and this immediately relieves the tension of buying shoes online. If the shoes don't fit, you can send them back. The company has 365-day return policy. That's right—you can wear the shoes for a year, decide you don't like them, and send them back.

You think that's the height of service? The Consumerist reported that a Zappos rep mailed, by overnight service, a free pair of shoes to a guy who was the best man at an out-of-town wedding who forgot his shoes!

Zappos prides itself on making connections with its customers and ensuring that its customers are raving fans. It is loyal to its customers, and the customers give it back in spades.

## Rule #6 Summary

Along with honesty, loyalty is the foundation of *The Howard Stern Show*. Howard has gained a loyalty among his listeners that is unrivaled by other fan groups, and that loyalty stems from his steadfast dedication to them.

He always put his fans first and never took them for granted. Because of his commitment to them, they followed him to satellite radio. Wouldn't you love to have customers who were willing to pay more for your service just because they love you?

You gain loyalty from your customers by providing them an experience that no one else can deliver and by making them feel as if they are part of something "bigger."

Celebrate your success with your customers; it helps to keep them engaged.

Connect with your customers and employees on an emotional level. Everyone in business is human, and we all want to satisfy our need for personal fulfillment.

If you build a loyal fan base, you have options that are not available to your competition. You can ask your fans to do things for you that others can't ask. Think Apple.

Suggested reading:
Brogan, Chris, and Julien Smith. *Trust Agents: Using the Web to Build Influence, Improve Reputation, and Earn Trust*. Hoboken, NJ: John Wiley & Sons, 2009.

Michelli, Joseph A. *The Zappos Experience: 5 Principles to Inspire, Engage, and Wow*. New York: McGraw-Hill, 2012.

# Rule #7: Demand Originality and Innovation

To say that Howard Stern is an original in the world of radio is like saying that Elvis was an original in the world of music. Howard defined a new genre of radio. He was like nothing that came before him, and he has left a trail of copycats and wannabes in his wake over the course of his career.

In a radio industry where even the most popular FM DJ's only spoke on air for a few minutes between songs, Howard had a plan to innovate. He talked in depth in his book *Private Parts* about how he felt that if he could entertain people in a meaningful way during their morning commutes, he had a chance to do something great. He knew that entertaining them meant much more than cheering them up between records. He needed to turn the common definition of radio on its ear.

In younger demographics, everyone was used to hearing songs during their commute.

He wanted to take their records away. He wanted to be a throwback to old-time radio where characters were developed and people tuned in to hear the next "chapter" of a never-ending soap opera.

Make no mistake—this was not "old-time radio." While every DJ in America was pleasant and cheery at all times, Howard told you how he really felt. Traditional DJs covered up the shortcomings or mistakes of their staff. Howard brought them to everyone's attention and made them part of the show.

Some radio shows tried to be all things to all people. Howard said of his show, "If you don't get it, don't listen, and leave me alone."

We live in a world where companies bottle water, one of our planet's most plentiful natural resources, and spend hundreds of millions of dollars to convince you that their water tastes better than another company's water.

Being an innovator is difficult, and it's much more art than science. There are some smart people who have taken on the task of trying to define than magical element that makes a brand unique. I had the pleasure of hearing Youngme Moon, the senior associate dean and chair of the MBA program at Harvard Business School, speak in support of her amazing book, *Different:*

*Escaping the Competitive Herd*. She spoke about the three elements that help a brand differentiate itself in a world of sameness. I encourage you to pick up a copy of the book if you want to understand how to differentiate yourself or your company in a crowded marketplace.

## Reverse-Position Brands

Reverse-position branding is not a *kama sutra* type of sex using hot pokers. According to Moon, reverse-position brands differentiate themselves not by continuously trying to out-do the competition by adding features but by taking features away.

Companies that use reverse positioning take away features that are often expected within the industry. They replace those features with elements that make for a new, different experience.

Moon cites JetBlue Airways as an example. JetBlue told its customers that there was no such thing as a free meal, so it didn't hand out meals. It did away with seat class (no first class, no coach, just seats). It did not discount tickets for round-trip flyers (all fares were based on one-way tickets).

JetBlue gave its customers an alternative experience. Every seat on the plane was leather, and it reclined more than most airline seats. The company offered competitive, almost discounted fares as well as something unheard of at the time: satellite televisions on every seat back.

Moon describes these brands as those that "say no where others say yes, but say yes where others say no."

Howard pulled the rug out from under many people when he did away with many of the staples of a traditional radio program. He took away the music, the traffic updates, the weather, and the time checks.

In return, he gave us more things that most listeners would not expect: a plethora of live, in–studio guests ranging from famous musicians to little-known porn stars. When musicians were in the studio, he gave us live, acoustic (before acoustic was cool) renditions of their most famous songs.

He often took his show on the road and broadcast live. Live broadcasts included everything from large gatherings of celebrities and fans for his famous birthday shows to broadcasting out of listeners' homes.

If everyone in an industry tries to be great at

everything, everyone is mediocre. Double down on your strengths more than trying to improve on your weaknesses. Your strengths will set you apart!

## Breakaway Brands

A breakaway brand turns preconceptions upside down. They differentiate themselves by placing themselves within a category and then breaking all the rules associated with that category. Once you can convince people to reclassify your product, you have the opportunity to create a breakout brand.

One example is Cirque du Soleil. Cirque Du Soleil is a circus only in the broadest of definition—there are no animals, clowns, or ringmasters. Much of the success associated with Cirque Du Soleil can be attributed to the fact that it was *billed* as a circus.

The odds are that a huge number of people who have seen Cirque Du Soleil would have never purchased a ticket if the show was billed as one that creatively combined gymnastics, dance, music, and theatre. Based on that description, guys like me would run for the exit.

I'm not sure about most other Stern fans, but I rarely think about Howard in terms of being a

DJ. He's accomplished and done things unlike any DJ before him.

Howard always refers to himself as a DJ and often compares himself to traditional DJs. It's important for him to classify himself as a DJ to help cement the fact that he is drastically different than any DJ ever. He is innovative and different compared to other DJ's, but what if he referred to himself as a comedian. As a comedian, Howard is extremely talented, but may not be the breakaway talent his is considered today. By comparing himself to DJs rather than comedians, the audience sees him as even more outrageous and unconventional.

## **Hostile Brands**

Hostile brands shout, "I am what I am! Take it or leave it!" Moon describes hostile brands in this way: "Instead of laying out the welcome mat, they lay down a gauntlet."

Hostile brand marketers understand that they are operating in a niche market and don't need to appeal to a mass market. Rather than trying to appeal to the masses, they try to shock, even offend, traditionalists.

By going after a niche of consumers who connect with their irreverence, they build a passionate following. These consumers help hostile brands build businesses that are often more powerful and profitable than traditional brands.

Traditional brands in large, mature markets are similar to their competition. The differences between one product and another are inconsequential. Consumers tend to drift toward and then away from the brands with little or no loyalty. They make their purchasing decisions based on factors like price and availability.

On the other hand, hostile brands playing in smaller niche markets have built such loyal customers that these consumers seek out the brand and don't consider others. This allows the brand to be more flexible in terms of pricing and offer more distribution options (it can afford to make its products more scarce). This adds up to a large piece of a smaller market with higher margins and more control over the supply chain.

Hostile brands appeal to the nonconformist. When the BMC Mini Cooper was released in the United States, the company not only embraced the car's size limitations but pushed them as a selling point to a population in love with Ford Explorers and Jeep Grand Cherokees. The nonconformists became brand loyalists.

Hostile brands say, "Try me if you dare," and people with the right disposition say, "Bring it on!"

Howard and hostility have long gone hand in hand. Howard pushes the boundaries of radio. He was fined hundreds of thousands of dollars by the FCC for violating decency acts and operating outside ethical standards. He talked on air about how he felt the fines and the FCC's interpretation of the rules were unfair, but these fines and the attention garnered helped cement his place in radio lore.

Hostility certainly surrounded Howard's 1992 comment about Alfred Sikes' cancer. Sikes was an FCC commissioner who had been in a bitter feud with Stern for many years. When Howard found out that Sikes had cancer, he made an on-air plea for the cancer to spread.

Nearly fifteen years later, in an interview with Ed Bradley on *60 Minutes*, he didn't apologize for the rant but did say it might not happen today. He said:

> *If you're going to be strong on the radio, you've got to let it all hang out—even the ugly stuff—and you can't apologize for it.*
> - Howard Stern on *60 Minutes* 12/2005

## Rule #7 Summary

Howard used every tactic in the book to separate himself from anyone he considered a competitor. He differentiated himself from the radio masses not by saying that he was different but by lumping himself in with a group of traditional radio DJs, knowing that he would smash the idea of what a DJ was to pieces. This was breakaway branding.

Howard established a niche of listeners by telling people that if they didn't like his show they should stop listening. He knew that his show would not appeal to everyone, but by saying so, he made more people want to see what he was up to. That is what hostile brands do best.

Howard took away the tenets of a morning radio show—weather, traffic, and time checks—and did his best to delight people on their morning commutes. He took away the expected and gave the unexpected, like any good reverse-position brand.

Innovation and differentiation are critical components to establishing your company and your brand.

If you watch what your competition is doing and copy it, you're heading toward a market that is marked by sameness and homogeny. Double down on your strengths rather than improving your weaknesses. Expanding your strength lengthens your lead against your competitors, but working on your weaknesses makes you more like everyone else.

Suggested reading:
Moon, Youngme. *Different: Escaping the Competitive Herd*. New York: Crown, 2010.

# Conclusion: An "Honest" Interview

Honesty is such an important element when it comes to both Howard Stern and building your business that I wanted to give you more information about its potential impact.

Larry Johnson, the coauthor of *Absolute Honesty*, was kind enough to grant me an interview so that I could dive into the concept of employing honesty in your business. The transcript of the interview follows. I didn't have time to conduct a full Howard Stern-type interview, so don't look for questions about Mr. Johnson's "johnson" or his salary or sexual relationships.

Jamie: From an organizational perspective, what are the biggest benefits for an organization that adopts a platform of honesty?

Larry: The biggest one from my perspective, and you know Bob and I based the book on our experiences over the last thirty years working as consultants inside offices, was that when there's this culture of honesty, where it's okay to be honest, even if it hurts somebody's feelings, where there's sort of an expectation that you be that way, a lot more information gets put on the table, which makes sense.

If you're sitting in a meeting and your boss is sitting there saying something that you know to be off track or not true, or maybe the whole picture isn't there, the culture says it's okay to say, "Hey, wait a minute boss, that's not the way I see it."

You probably know, having read the book, that one of the laws is disagree and commit, which we took from Intel. There's sort of this expectation in the culture that you disagree if you don't agree. That doesn't mean you get your way, but it says you are expected to say something. Once a decision is made, then go along with it. Commit.

Jamie: What tools can companies and teams use to ensure that employees give and receive honest feedback from their peers and their bosses?

Larry: Specific tools? When you say that, I'm thinking that all the kind of tools that a company will use to change the culture in any direction are the same kinds of tools you use to build a culture of honesty. That would be certainly a complete and public executive embracement of honesty.

Jamie: So it's really top down?

Larry: Yes, it has to be top down, because I am not going to go out on a limb and be honest if I don't know that that's okay.

Jamie: They kill the messenger?

Larry: Yeah, then the messenger gets killed, and we have naked emperors. So the folks with the power need to make sure that everyone down below them knows that it's okay to be honest, to be frank, to express a different opinion, and I'm not going to get burnt for it.

In fact, if anyone is going to get burned, it's the one who doesn't speak up, then complains about what's going on. I don't know if you've ever been to a meeting where people will sit there and nod their heads during a meeting, or they do speak up, but then once [the issue is] settled, they don't say much more. Then they go out the door and complain. The real meeting takes place in the parking lot where people whine.

I know Intel does this, and this is the model we took, that one way to create a cultural standard is to publish it and then practice it. It's like when companies say "the customers come first" or any other cultural standard. It starts out with a lot of publication and a lot of training. That gives people the tools, for example, to disagree with someone in a productive way. And then there is the matter of supporting it, and that's really where the rubber meets the road.

If you celebrate being an iconoclast and being odd man out, and it's okay coming up with off-the-reservation ideas or whatever it happens to be, that people don't get chopped off at the knees for doing so, and that's sort of a tool of changing the culture.

You establish what the rules are and what the new culture is going to look like, and you publish that on a regular basis. Then when push comes to shove, you walk the walk.

Jamie: Transparency is a word that we hear a lot lately, particularly with [the] recent financial meltdown on Wall Street. Do you see there being a big difference between transparency and honesty when it comes to culture, or are they same thing?

Larry: I think they're linked. Transparency means you need to be honest and open about what goes behind decisions, that you are sort of open about the way you do business, but you don't have to be transparent to be honest. Let's face it. There are some things you don't want to be transparent about like company secrets. That's a different kind of corporate culture, too.

Some companies are a whole lot more transparent than others, and it's okay for all their employees to know the company secret stuff, because they say, "Well, we trust our employees not to share it." Some companies don't do that. Coca-Cola probably trusts their employees, but they don't pass out their secret formula to everyone in the organization!

Jamie: You speak a lot about Intel's culture of honesty in your book, but you don't necessarily think honest when you think of Intel. Have you come across companies that make honesty the cornerstone of their public persona?

Larry: In the book, we use Johnson & Johnson as one of our standard bearers of being an honest and open culture. Unfortunately, they just got in trouble here a while back for the very reasons that we kind of cited as "that's how companies get in trouble." They had some problems with the quality of their products, and they did exactly what they didn't do with Tylenol.

That sort of changes with management and what management does. Other companies where we saw that kind of culture, but not necessarily as formalized, were Harley Davidson and American Express.

Jamie: What are the biggest mistakes that companies will make when trying to build a culture of honesty?

Larry: (chuckles) They do dishonest things.

Jamie: So it really comes down to them not holding true to principles?

Larry: Yeah, more than anything else, it kind of comes down to the company philosophy. For example, we might say we are dedicated to quality, or we are dedicated to "doing the right thing," then when push comes to shove, we need to get product out the door, whether it's a quality product or not. The manager on the floor makes a decision that "We are just going to get it out the door regardless of whether it's been inspected or not. " It's that idea of "what do the managers do on a daily basis" that demonstrates that we are a company that always does the right thing. If we are a company, for example, who advertises that we are concerned with the planet or green, but we don't do anything to reduce our waste or to reduce our carbon footprint, we just sort of give lip service to it. You know, employees see right through that real quick.

Jamie: So it's honesty by example?

Larry: Always. It comes down to things like who gets promoted. Is it the person who is respected and does the right thing and is respected for doing the right thing? Or is it the guy who kisses ass or gets ahead by doing the wrong things or not by practicing the code that the company professes?

Jamie: We've talked a lot about how honesty influences relationships internally. How does honesty extend to vendors or customers?

Larry: How you treat your customers or vendors can say a lot. I've only heard this so I don't know this to be absolutely true, but I've heard from more than one source that does business with Wal-Mart that they treat their vendors a whole lot differently than they treat their customers.

Like anything else, that can affect your reputation. A lot of honesty is tied to reputation. If you are doing the right thing and being honest with people and straight with them, and treating them fairly and in a way that can be respected, that word gets around. Likewise, and I know that this is the case with Wal-Mart, how they treat their employees has caused them a lot of bad press especially when it comes to things like healthcare.

Jamie: Do employees in companies with a culture of honesty have higher job satisfaction? Do they feel like they are more part of a team?

What does it do for the individual employee in terms of how they approach their job every day?

Larry: Well, the research quoted in the book—we found a study that found that employees tend to be happier and turnover tends to be lower in companies where they have a clearly defined standard of ethics and honesty, so just taking from that study, you tend to have happier employees. It just makes sense. People want to work with people they feel are honest and above board, and if they don't, I don't know that I particularly want them working for me.

Jamie: Are there cases where you have come across an organization that can't even be honest with itself?

Larry: I think Enron was a good example of that. Ken Lay, well, I don't know if he believed what he was saying. They did have some standards of accounting practices that were published, but it was interesting. In 1997, they made a conscious decision to abandon those practices. Not sure I'm answering your question, but they were a company that consciously decided to not abide by standards that most companies should abide by.

Jamie: I know that this was outside the

scope of your book, but did you ever explore the correlation between honesty and how honesty affected advertising and marketing? How companies build trust in the marketplace by being honest and authentic?

Larry: You're right, we didn't get into that, we focused more on corporate culture, but it makes sense to me that when you're honest in what you advertise and deliver on what you say, that people come to trust you.

Jamie: What you hear today—particularly as it relates to social media, in terms of building brand and establishing value in addition to having a good product or service to sell—is that it's extremely important to be authentic when approaching a market. Consumers can very quickly sniff out when you're not being authentic.

Larry: Yeah, well, it's not only that they can sniff it out. They can communicate it in ways they never could before. You know, you burn a customer twenty years ago, and the research shows that he would tell eleven other people about it. Being burned now? If you burn him bad enough, he'll go online and tell thousands. He'll tell everybody in his Facebook network. It's almost swung to the other side—there are some customers who have unrealistic expectations or are just kind of crazy. So they want something really unreasonable, and you do everything you can to make it right for them, and you try to be nice, but it's just off the charts, and they can do the same thing to you.

Jamie: That's where you get into reputation management.

Larry: Yeah, and it's tough. It's a whole new world out there, as most people know, with the Internet. I can publish anything I want. I can be vindictive if I want. Maybe somebody in that company stole my girlfriend, so I'm going to get them.

Jamie: Well, Mr. Johnson, I want to thank you for your time, and I want you to know that I've really enjoyed your book and the videos that I've managed to get my hands on of you when you present.

Larry: Great. I would love to know when your book comes out. I'd like to read it.

Jamie: I will send you an advance copy as soon as it comes off the press.

# About the Author

Jamie Troia is CEO and founder of Greystack Inbound Marketing, a new breed marketing agency that helps businesses transform the way they market to their customers on the Internet.

Jamie went to Siena College, and has been involved in technology and marketing since the early days of the web.

In his spare time, he runs his kids to sporting events, follows the trifecta of the Yankees, Giants and Rangers, collects and occasionally drinks small batch bourbon, and toggles his Sirius radio between *Howard 100* and *The Grateful Dead Channel*.

# Resources

The following resources have been referenced or were invaluable when writing this book:

Brogan, Chris, and Julien Smith. *Trust Agents: Using the Web to Build Influence, Improve Reputation, and Earn Trust*. Hoboken, NJ: John Wiley & Sons, 2009. Print.

Colford, Paul D. *Howard Stern: King of All Media : The Unauthorized Biography*. New York: St. Martin's, 1996. Print.

Collins, James C. *Good to Great: Why Some Companies Make the Leap--and Others Don't*. New York, NY: HarperBusiness, 2001. Print.

Dell'Abate, Gary, and Chad Millman. *They Call Me Baba Booey*. New York: Spiegel & Grau, 2010. Print.

Gladwell, Malcolm. *The Tipping Point: How Little Things Can Make a Big Difference*. Boston: Little, Brown, 2000. Print.

Godin, Seth. *Purple Cow: Transform Your Business by Being Remarkable*. New York: Portfolio, 2003. Print.

Johnson, Larry, and Bob Phillips. *Absolute Honesty: Building a Corporate Culture That Values Straight Talk and Rewards Integrity*. New York: AMACOM, American Management Association, 2003. Print.

Linkner, Josh. *Disciplined Dreaming: A Proven System to Drive Breakthrough Creativity*. San Francisco: Jossey-Bass, 2011. Print.

Michelli, Joseph A. The Zappos Experience: 5 Principles to Inspire, Engage, and Wow. New York: McGraw-Hill, 2012. Print.

Moon, Youngme. *Different: Escaping the Competitive Herd.* New York: Crown, 2010. Print.

Stern, Howard. *Miss America.* New York: Regan, 1995. Print.

Stern, Howard. *Private Parts.* New York: Simon & Schuster, 1993. Print.

Tracy, Brian. *Full Engagement!: Inspire, Motivate, and Bring out the Best in Your People.* New York: American Management Association, 2011. Print.

Vaynerchuk, Gary. *Crush It!: Why Now Is the Time to Cash in on Your Passion.* [New York]: HarperStudio, 2009. Print.

"Howard Stern Talks with Sean Hannity." *Hannity & Colmes.* Fox News. 07 Mar. 2005. Television.

"Howard Stern Enters the No Spin Zone." *The O'Reilly Factor.* Fox News. 7-9 Dec. 2005. Television.

"Howard Stern's New Challenge." *60 Minutes.* 4 Dec. 2005. Television. Transcript.

Too numerous to mention. *The Howard Stern Show.* Radio.

Helm, Burt, and Tom Lowry. "Blasting Away at Product Placement." *Business Week* 15 Oct. 2009: Web.

Clifford, Stephanie. "A Product's Place Is on the Set." *The New York Times* 22 July 2008:

Ben Sisario "Howard Stern Sues Sirius XM Radio, Saying It Reneged on Stock Awards" *The New York Times*, March 22, 2011

Associated Press, *"Sirius gives Howard Stern $83 million bonus"*, NBCNews.com, 1/9/2007, Web.

Ben Popken, "*Zappos Saves Best Man From Going Barefoot At Wedding*", May 19, 2011 The Consumerist, Web.
Geoffrey A. Fowler and Jessica A. Vascellar, "Hype Hangs Over Dropbox", *The Wall Street Journal*, April 3, 2012. Web WSJ.com

Strauss, Neill. "The Long Neurotic Triumph of Howard Stern: The Happiest Man Alive. *"Rolling Stone* 31 Mar. 2011

Made in the USA
Columbia, SC
08 December 2017